1G PA

K21
/15   Δ4135

The Book of Letters of Saint Patrick the Bishop

LIBER EPISTOLARUM
SANCTI PATRICII EPISCOPI

THE
BOOK OF LETTERS OF
SAINT PATRICK
THE BISHOP

Edited and Translated
with Analysis and Commentary by

D. R. HOWLETT

FOUR COURTS PRESS

This book was set in
10.5 on 12pt Bembo
by Seton Music Graphics Ltd,
Gurtycloona, Bantry, Co. Cork, for
FOUR COURTS PRESS LTD
Kill Lane, Blackrock, Co. Dublin.

and, in North America,
FOUR COURTS PRESS LTD
c/o International Specialized Book Series,
5804 NE Hassalo Street, Portland, OR 97213.

ISBN 1-85182-136-8
ISBN 1-85182-137-6 pbk

A catalogue record for this book
is available for the British Library.

Printed in Ireland by Colour Books Ltd., Dublin

Margaretae tutrici et collegae Margaretae

Oute of oryent I hardyly saye
Ne proued I neuer her precios pere

PREFACE

In thanking friends and colleagues who have helped me to read and understand the works of St Patrick and to bring this little book to publication pleasure coincides with duty. To Michael Adams, Dr John Blundell, Kieran Devine, Dr Anthony Harvey, Dr Leofranc Holford-Strevens, Professor Donnchadh Ó Corráin, Sister Máire Bríd de Paor, Dr Richard Sharpe, and the Librarians of the Royal Irish Academy I owe varied debts acknowledged with gratitude. Older and deeper debts are acknowledged in the dedication to Marguerite Ephron, Professor emerita of Latin and my undergraduate adviser at the University of Montana, and Margaret Bent, F.B.A., Fellow of All Souls College, Oxford.

CONTENTS

INTRODUCTION

Engagement with the works of St Patrick has provided a wonderful form of play, in which three lines of interest have converged: ancestral ties with the *parochia Patricii*, professional association with the Royal Irish Academy's *Dictionary of Medieval Latin from Celtic Sources*, and intense private pleasure in learning to listen to the words of a great saint.

If Patrick was a *homo unius libri* 'a man of one book', he had read, marked, learned, and inwardly digested that book. He appropriated not only the words, but the inner meanings and habits of thought he had found in the Latin Bible and internalized them to a remarkable degree, as we shall see both in his quotations from and allusions to Biblical texts and in his structuring of narrative.

Patrick's *Epistola* and *Confessio* are dense compositions not only filled with delights for the ears, eyes, and minds of the attentive, but armed with defences against careless reproduction, incompetent editing, and ignorant reading by the insensitive. Modern scholars, by ignoring the defences, have missed many of the delights. They have taken at face value Patrick's apparent confessions of ignorance and inelegance, conveying to modern readers a notion that he was an incoherent thinker and inarticulate writer, who could 'give an impression of spluttering incoherence'[1] and refer to his own prose as 'drivel'.[2] The greatest modern editor of the works of Patrick has stated that 'the apostle of the Irish was not a *littérateur*'[3] and complained of his 'naive rhetoric'[4] and 'the vagueness of structure that is so characteristic of his style'[5] and his 'constant struggle with the language, and a rather involved way of thinking'.[6] Professor Carney has judged him 'an

---

1 A. B. E. Hood (ed. & transl.), *St Patrick, His Writings and Muirchu's Life*, History from the Sources (London & Chichester, 1978) p. 18.
2 C. H. H. Wright (transl.), *The Writings of St Patrick*, Christian Classics Series VI (3rd ed. enlarged, London, n.d.) p. 49.
3 L. Bieler (ed.), *Libri Epistolarum Sancti Patricii Episcopi, Classica et Mediaevalia* XI (1950) p. 5. *Cf. ibid.* p. 28: 'The apostle of Ireland was not a man of letters'.
4 *Idem, The Life and Legend of St. Patrick, Problems of Modern Scholarship* (Dublin, 1949) p. 73.
5 *Idem, Libri* XI p. 44.
6 *Idem, Life and Legend* p. 49.

inexperienced writer',[7] and Professor Binchy has described him as the 'simple Patrick of the Confessio', a writer of 'stumbling barbarous Latin'.[8] Bishop Patrick Hanson, one of the most sensible and sensitive students of Patrick's life and work, has stated that

> Patrick ... could not conduct a sustained argument in Latin. He could not carry through a narrative in a well-ordered way. He had no literary devices, no store of syntactical variations, no reserves of vocabulary, no art at all, in using Latin.[9]

Again:

> Patrick's writing is completely devoid of rhetoric. ... Patrick was incapable of writing for effect. It was all he could do to convey his thoughts to the reader without artifice, and even then he was not always able to do that.[10]

Such scholars have grievously misunderstood and grotesquely misrepresented Patrick by not attending to the lexical connections of his thought. In an attempt to correct this misapprehension the following Latin texts are arranged *per cola et commata* 'by clauses and phrases', to reveal the units of Patrick's thought. The accompanying English translation follows, wherever possible, line for line, mood for mood, voice for voice, word for word, including every *idcirco, ideoque, igitur, itaque, quidem, scilicet, tamen,* and *utique.* It attempts to distinguish *ait, dicit, inquit,* and *locutus est,* and to represent in English the underlying etymological connections of the Latin words, rendering *grauiter* 'oppressively' and *grauitudinem* 'oppressiveness'; *docere* 'to teach', *docui* 'I have taught', *indoctus* 'untaught', not 'unlearned'; *miser* 'pitiable', not 'wretched', *miserissime* 'most pitiably', *misericordia* 'pity', not 'mercy'; *testatur* 'he testifies', *testificor* 'I bear testimony', *testimonium* 'testimony', *testis* 'testifier', not 'witness'. This may produce inelegant translation, but it enables readers of English to note Patrick's repetition of words and ideas, the significance of which will emerge in the analysis. Only after apprehending the mechanical structure of Patrick's thought and prose can one begin to hear the tenor of his explicit statements and the undertones and overtones of his implicit resonances.

We may take as a model for such composition the vision of the Prophet Ezekiel, a captive, like Patrick, in a foreign land, where he saw *et aspectus*

7 J. Carney, *The Problem of St. Patrick* (Dublin, 1961) p. 94.
8 D. A. Binchy, 'Patrick and His Biographers Ancient and Modern', *Studia Hibernica* II (1962) pp. 55, 143.
9 R. P. C. Hanson, *Saint Patrick: His Origins and Career* (Oxford, 1968) p. 163.
10 *Idem* (transl.), *The Life and Writings of the Historical Saint Patrick* (New York, 1983) p. 36.

earum et opera quasi sit rota in medio rotae 'both their appearance and working as if it were a wheel in the middle of a wheel', like the inclusion of a chiastic sentence within a chiastic paragraph, itself within a chiastic chapter which is part of a chiastic whole. In the account of his sixth vision Patrick describes being within his own body and yet looking down upon someone else praying within him and also hearing the Holy Spirit praying above his interior man. As the Holy Spirit spoke to Patrick so he speaks to us, through and within and around his narrative, in harmonies that grow more complex, with resonances that reverberate longer, through meanings that become richer and denser every time we return to his texts.

It would be impertinent to try to rescue the works of Patrick from the state into which traditions of misdirected and acrimonious modern scholarship have brought them unless the Apostle of the Irish had provided the means. By listening to him on his own terms we can hear him speak articulately, authoritatively, compellingly, across fifteen centuries, with a power he believed to be not his own but God's.

Professor Ludwig Bieler established the text of Patrick's literary works in a justly famous edition, published with introduction, critical apparatus, and commentary in *Classica et Mediaevalia* XI (1950) and XII (1951),[11] reprinted as *Libri Epistolarum Sancti Patricii Episcopi* by the Irish Manuscripts Commission (Dublin: Stationery Office, 1952). In 1989 the Royal Irish Academy published as the third volume in a series ancillary to the *Dictionary of Medieval Latin from Celtic Sources* the *Clavis Patricii I, A Computer-Generated Concordance to the 'Libri Epistolarum' of Saint Patrick*, by Kieran Devine with a foreword by Anthony Harvey, based upon Bieler's edition, which is to be reprinted with a bibliography by Dr Harvey in the same series as *Clavis Patricii II* and *III*. As these excellent works are readily accessible there is no need to reproduce their apparatus, commentary, indices, or bibliography.

---

11 See also L. Bieler (transl.), *The Works of St. Patrick, St. Secundinus Hymn on St. Patrick*, Ancient Christian Writers, The Works of the Fathers in Translation (Westminster MD & London, 1953).

PATRICK'S TEXT

The text of Patrick's *Epistola* and *Confessio* presented here follows Bieler's text with a few changes, only three of them mine (the verb *obiecerunt* in 26, the pronoun *me* in 29, and the adverb *crebre* in 35), all the others attested among the variant readings and editorial conjectures recorded in the apparatus of Bieler's edition. Forms differing only in orthography from those of Bieler's text are all correct Classical spellings, most justified both from extant manuscripts and from analogy with examples elsewhere in Bieler's text.

Epistola

(2) for *in numero* read *innumerum numerum*.
(7) for *crudeliter <per> paenitentiam* read *crudeliter paenitentiam*.
(10) for *decorione* read *decurione*.

Confessio

(1) for †*bannauem taburniae*† read *Bannauenta Berniae*.
(1) for *qui <nos> nostram salutem* read *qui nostram salutem*.
(4) for *nec umquam fuit nec ante nec erit post haec* read *nec umquam fuit ante nec erit post haec*.
(4) for *apud Patrem <et> inenarrabiliter genitum* read *apud Patrem inenarrabiliter genitum*.
(4) for *effudit in nobis habunde* read *effudit in nobis abunde*.
(9) for *ne incederem in linguam* read *ne inciderem in linguam*.
(10) for *quia desertis breuitate* read *quia disertis breuitate*.
(11) for *deserta sed* †*ratum et fortissimum*† *scripta* read *diserta sed rata et fortissima scripta*.
(13) for *Vnde autem ammiramini itaque magni et pusilli qui timetis Deum et uos dominicati rethorici audite et scrutamini. Quis ...* read *Vnde autem admiramini itaque magni et pusilli qui timetis Deum et uos domini cati rethorici audite ergo et scrutamini quis ... .*
(14) for *exaga<e>llias* read *exagallias*.
(18) for *ut uenirem ad tegoriolum* read *ut uenirem ad teguriolum*.
(19) for *ubique habundabat illi* read *ubique abundabat illi*.

(19) for *canes eorum repleti sunt* read *carne eorum repleti sunt.*

(19) for *cibum habundanter habuerunt* read *cibum abundanter habuerunt.*

(23) for *Victoricus* read *Uictoricius.*

(24) for *uerbis peritissime* read *uerbis peritissimis.*

(24) for *sic expertus sum* read *sic expergefactus sum.*

(25) for *stupebam et ammirabam* read *stupebam et admirabam.*

(26) after *peccata mea contra laboriosum episcopatum meum* supply *obiecerunt.*

(29) for *uidi … scriptum erat contra faciem* read *uidi … quod scriptum erat contra faciem.*

(29) for *quasi sibi se iunxisset* read *quasi sibi me iunxisset.*

(34) for *mihi †tanta diuinitate cooperasti†* read *mihi tanta diuinitate comparuisti.*

(35) for *pupillum ideo tamen responsum diuinum creber admonere* read *pupillum idiotam responsum diuinum crebre admonere.*

(37) for *aliquantis de senioribus* read *aliquantos de senioribus.*

(39) for *Abraam* read *Abraham.*

(40) for *ammonet et docet* read *admonet et docet* .

(42) for *Sed ex illis maxime laborabant* read *Sed et illae maxime laborabant.*

(43) for *usque ad Gallias uisitare frates* read *usque ad Gallias uisitare fratres.*

(46) for *pos tergum meum narrabant* read *post tergum meum narrabant.*

(51) for *omnia <…> generaui* read *omnia generaui.*

(57) for *scrutator corda et renes* read *scrutatur corda et renes.*

Biblical quotations are enclosed within single inverted commas. Direct discourse is enclosed within double inverted commas.

PATRICK'S STYLE

In the following arrangement of the *Epistola* and the *Confessio* the lines of text exhibit the nature of St Patrick's thought, expressed *per cola et commata* 'by clauses and phrases', in iterative or antiphonal statement and restatement, as found in the Latin Bible. A good example in parallel order is Isaiah 1 10:

```
       a        b          c         d            e
    audite  uerbum  Domini  principes  Sodomorum
                       a'          b'  c'           d'        e'
    percipite auribus  legem Dei nostri populus Gomorrae.
       a        b            c        d          e
    Hear the word of the Lord, princes of the Sodomites.
                          a'        b'        c'      d'         e'
    Perceive with ears the law of our God, people of Gomorrah.
```

A good example in chiastic order is Lamentations 1 1:

```
         a i           a ii
    facta est quasi uidua      a    She has been made like a widow
       b i      b ii
    domina gentium             b    the lady among the gentiles;
    b'i          b'ii
    princeps prouinciarum  b'       the princess among the provinces
       a'i        a'ii
    facta est sub tributo      a'   has been made tributary.
```

A good example of a larger unit, which extends to several verses, combining parallelism, represented by the italic letters in the right column, and chiasmus, represented by the roman letters in the left column, is Amos II 14–6:

```
    a   a     et peribit fuga a ueloce
    b   b         et fortis non obtinebit uirtutem suam
    c   c            et robustus non saluabit animam suam
    d   d              et tenens arcum non stabit
    d'  a'              et uelox pedibus suis non saluabitur
    c'  b'            et ascensor equi non saluabit animam suam
    b'  c'         et robustus corde inter fortes
    a'  d'     nudus fugiet in die illa dicit Dominus.
```

a	*a*	and flight will perish from the swift one
b	*b*	and the strong one will not retain his own power
c	*c*	and the robust will not save his own soul
d	*d*	and the one holding the bow will not stand
d'	*a'*	and the one swift in his own feet will not be saved
c'	*b'*	and the mounter of the horse will not save his own soul
b'	*c'*	and the robust in heart among the strong ones
a'	*d'*	will flee away naked in that day, says the Lord.

To establish a chiastic pattern the word *fuga* in a is balanced by *fugiet* in a'; the same concluding phrase appears in both c and c', *non saluabit animam suam*; similar concluding phrases appear in d and d', *non stabit* and *non saluabitur*, and the last words of b', *inter fortes*, echo the first words of b, *et fortis*. To establish a parallel pattern the last words of *a*, *a ueloce*, are balanced by the first words of *a'*, *et uelox*; and the words *et robustus* are repeated at the beginnings of *c* and *c'*.

The patterns exhibit balance not only in the statement and restatement of ideas, but in the numbers of words and syllables and letters. These are arranged usually in one of two forms, either perfect symmetry or division by extreme and mean ratio, the golden section.[12] In the former there are exactly as many words or syllables or letters in one part as in the other. In the latter the number in the minor part (m) relates to the number in the major part (M) as the number in the major part relates to the number in the whole (m+M): $m/M = M/(m+M)$. To calculate the major part one could multiply a number by 0.61803, and to calculate the minor part one could multiply a number by 0.38197.

Or one could compile a table of Fibonacci numbers, each of which is the sum of the two to its left.

---

12 Euclid dealt with extreme and mean ratio in Book II proposition xi and Book VI proposition xxx of the *Elements*. See T. L. Heath (transl.), *The Thirteen Books of Euclid's Elements* ed. 2 (Cambridge, 1956) vol. I p. 137 and H. L. L. Busard (ed.), *The First Latin Translation of Euclid's 'Elements' Commonly Ascribed to Adelard of Bath* Pontifical Institute of Mediaeval Studies, Studies and Texts LXIV (Toronto, 1983). See also Boethius *De Institutione Arithmetica* II LII. F. Lasserre, *The Birth of Mathematics in the Age of Plato* (Larchmont NY, 1964). H. E. Huntley, *The Divine Proportion, A Study in Mathematical Beauty* (New York, 1970). R. Herz-Fischler, *A Mathematical History of Division in Extreme and Mean Ratio* (Waterloo Ont., 1987).

1	1	2	3	5	8	13	21	34	55	89	144	233
1	2	3	5	8	13	21	34	55	89	144	233	377
1	3	4	7	11	18	29	47	76	123	199	322	521
1	4	5	9	14	23	37	60	97	157	254	411	665
1	5	6	11	17	28	45	73	118	191	309	500	809
1	6	7	13	20	33	53	86	139	225	364	589	953
1	7	8	15	23	38	61	99	160	259	419	678	1097
1	8	9	17	26	43	69	112	181	293	474	767	1241
1	9	10	19	29	48	77	125	202	327	529	856	1385
1	10	11	21	32	53	85	138	223	361	584	945	1529
1	11	12	23	35	58	93	151	244	395	639	1034	1673
1	12	13	25	38	63	101	164	265	429	694	1123	1817

A writer who consults such a table sees that if he has composed a passage of eighty-nine words and wants its pair to exhibit extreme and mean ratio he must compose either fifty-five or 144 words.

Another way to calculate extreme and mean ratio is, as Dr John Blundell suggests, to divide a number successively by 2 and 3.

$n = 100$		$n = 196$		$n = 228$	
÷2 50	+ 50	÷2 98	+ 98	÷2 114	+ 114
÷2 25		÷2 49		÷2 57	
÷2 12½	+ 12½	÷2 24½	+ 24½	÷2 28½	+ 28½
÷2 6¼		÷2 12¼		÷2 14¼	
÷3 2 $^{1}/_{12}$		÷3 $^{49}/_{12}$		÷3 $^{57}/_{12}$	
÷3 $^{25}/_{36}$	− $^{25}/_{36}$	÷3 $^{49}/_{36}$	− 1 $^{13}/_{36}$	÷3 1 $^{21}/_{36}$	− 1 $^{21}/_{36}$
= 61 $^{29}/_{36}$		= 121 $^{5}/_{36}$		= 140 $^{11}/_{36}$	

This form of calculation is equivalent to multiplication by 89/144.[13]

The reason for mathematical composition of literary texts is that a writer imitates in his composition what he believes God to have done in the world. Two famous passages of the Old Testament and another in the Apocrypha present God's creation as a mathematical act of weighing, measuring, and balancing. In Job XXXVIII 4-7 God asks

ubi eras quando ponebam
fundamenta terrae?

Where were you when I laid the
foundations of the earth?

13 The number 144, which recurs frequently in the following analyses, may have been symbolically important to Patrick as the square of the number 12 (the number of tribes of Israel and the number of apostles) and the twelfth number in what we know as the Fibonacci series, as well as the number of cubits in the wall of the heavenly Jerusalem, the inhabitants of which numbered 144,000 (Apocalypse XXI 17 and VII 4).

indica mihi si habes
intellegentiam
  quis
    posuit
      mensuras eius
si nosti
  uel quis
    tetendit
      super eam lineam
      super quo bases illius
    solidatae sunt
  aut quis
    dimisit
      lapidem angularem eius
cum me laudarent simul astra
matutina
et iubilarent omnes filii Dei.

Tell me, if you have
understanding.
  Who
    laid
      its measurements,
if you know?
  Or who
    stretched
      the line upon it?
      Upon what are its bases
    grounded,
or who
  laid down
    its corner stone
when the morning stars praised me
together
and all the sons of God shouted for
joy.

Again in Isaiah XL 12 the prophet says that it is God

quis mensus est
  pugillo
    aquas
      et
    caelos
  palmo
ponderauit
quis adpendit
  tribus digitis
    molem terrae
et librauit
  in pondere
    montes
      et
    colles
  in statera.

Who has measured
  in the hollow of His hand
    the waters
      and
    the heavens
  in His palm
weighed
Who has suspended
  with three fingers
    the bulk of the earth
and balanced
  with a weight
    the mountains
      and
    the hills
  with a steelyard.

Yet again in Sapientia XI 21 'Solomon' addressing the Creator says *sed omnia mensura et numero et pondere disposuisti* 'but You have disposed all things by measure and number and weight'. This arithmetic exactness extends also to the New Testament, in which Jesus states in Matthew X 30 *uestri autem et capilli capitis omnes numerati sunt* 'but even the hairs of your head are all numbered'.

There is explicit discussion in the Talmud of the counting of verses, words, and letters of the text of the Hebrew Bible.[14] In a dialogue which continued to be read in the Latin West Plato makes Timaeus discuss in minute particulars the mathematical creation of the world.[15]

In the texts mentioned above note that Isaiah 1 10 has five words in the first part and seven words in the second part, together twelve, which divides by extreme and mean ratio at 7 and 5. Lamentations 1 1 has four words in part a and four words in part a', two words in part b and two words in part b'.

A good example from the New Testament is the Prologue to St John's Gospel.

A1	In principio	In the beginning
2	erat	was
3	Uerbum	the Word
4	et Uerbum	and the Word
5	erat	was
6	apud Deum	with God
7	et	and
6'	Deus	God
5'	erat	was
4'	Uerbum;	the Word;
3'	Hoc	He
2	erat	was
1'	in principio apud Deum.	in the beginning with God.
B1	Omnia	All things
2	per ipsum facta sunt	through Him were made
3	et	and
2'	sine ipso factum est	without Him was made
1'	nihil.	nothing.
C1	Quod factum est in ipso	What was made in Him
2	uita erat	was life
3	et	and
2'	uita erat	the life was
1'	lux hominum.	the light of men.
D1	Et lux in tenebris lucet	And the light shines in the shadows
1'	et tenebrae eam non comprehenderunt.	and the shadows have not overcome it.

14 Rabbi Dr H. Freedman (transl.), *Kiddushin* ch. 1 30a-30b, in Rabbi Dr I. Epstein (ed.), *The Babylonian Talmud: Seder Nashim* (London, 1936) vol. VIII pp. 144-6.

15 Plato *Timaeus* §§ 31-32. For a Latin translation see J. H. Waszink (ed.), *Timaeus a Calcidio Translatus Commentarioque Instructus* in R. Klibansky (ed.) *Corpus Platonicum Medii Aevi* (London & Leiden, 1962) pp. 24-5. For specific discussion of the creation of the world by extreme and mean ratio see F. M. Cornford, *Plato's Cosmology* (London, 1937) p. 45.

In Jerome's Vulgate translation of this Prologue there are nineteen words in A, arranged, nine, one, nine; thirty-seven syllables, arranged eighteen, one, eighteen; eighty-three letters, arranged forty-one, two, forty. In B there are eleven words, arranged five, one, five; nineteen syllables, arranged nine, one, nine; forty-six letters, arranged twenty-two, two, twenty-two. In C there are twelve words arranged eight, four. There are twenty syllables, arranged twelve, eight. The golden section of 20 falls at 12 and 8. There are forty-seven letters, arranged twenty-nine, eighteen. The golden section of 47 falls at 29 and 18. In D there are five words in the first clause and five in the second. There are eight syllables in the first clause and twelve in the second, the golden section of 20 falling at 12 and 8. There are twenty letters in the first clause and thirty-one in the second, the golden section of 51 falling at 31.5 and 19.5.

God is mentioned three times (3×1). The first example *Deum* is the ninth word (3×3). From the first *Deum* to the second *Deus* inclusive there are three words (3×1). From the second *Deus* to the third *Deum* inclusive there are nine words (3×3). After that there are thirty-three words (3×11) to the end of the Prologue. The verb *facere* appears three times, first as *facta*, the fourth word (4×1) of part B. Between the first *facta* and the second *factum* there are four words. After *factum* the fourth word is *factum*, after which there are twenty words (4×5) to the end of the Prologue. The fourth word after *factum* is *uita*. From *uita* to *uita* inclusive there are four words. From *lux* to *lux* inclusive there are four words. From *tenebris* to *tenebrae* inclusive there are four words, and *tenebrae* is the fourth word from the end of the Prologue.

The account of the perfection of Sabbath rest after the Creation in Genesis II 1-4 contains forty-six Hebrew words. The Vulgate text of the account of Creation in Job XXXVIII 4-7 contains forty-six Latin words. The numerical value of the Greek letters in the name of God's creature AΔAM is $1+4+1+40 = 46$. As men's works should reflect God's work it took forty-six years to build the Temple in Jerusalem (John II 20). So in the Greek text of John I 3, the account of Creation by Christ, there are forty-six letters. There are also forty-six letters in the Latin text of that passage.

Sometimes Patrick states and restates an idea within a single line, as *Epistola* 7 *sed cogor zelo Dei et ueritas Xpisti excitauit*, with four words in each clause. Sometimes he makes pairs of adjacent lines, as 40-1 *non usurpo, partem habeo*, with two words in each line, or 74-5 *'Qui odit fratrem suum homicida' adscribitur, uel 'Qui non diligit fratrem suum in morte manet'*, with six words in the first line and nine words in the second, together fifteen, of which the golden section falls at 9 and 6. Sometimes he writes a doublet in one line followed by a singlet in the next line, as 15-6 *non dico ciuibus meis neque ciuibus sanctorum Romanorum, sed ciuibus daemoniorum ob mala opera ipsorum*, or 27-8 *an qui interfecti uel quos ceperunt, uel quos grauiter zabulus inlaqueauit*. Sometimes he quotes a chiastic passage from the Bible and expands it, as 60-5:

a   'Diuitias' inquit 'quas congregauit iniuste euomentur de uentre eius.

b   trahit illum angelus mortis.

c   ira draconum

d   mulcabitur.

d'   interficiet illum

c'   lingua colubris.

b'   comedit autem eum ignis inextinguibilis.'

a'   Ideoque 'Uae qui replent se quae non sunt sua.'

The text of a–b' derives from the Septuagint version of Job XX 15, and the text of a' from Habakkuk II 6. Patrick adds *inquit* to a, as he adds *ideoque* to a'; both verses allude to taking things for oneself unjustly. Dire punishments are threatened in b and b' in present tense verbs. The 'wrath of dragons' in c is balanced by the 'tongue of a serpent' in c'. The verbs at the crux in d and d' are future tense. This form of composition is so clear throughout Patrick's writings as to require no further analysis here.

I have marked Patrick's rhythms both clausular or quantitative and cursus or stressed. The subject of Latin prose rhythm is complicated and hotly debated, but few scholars would deny the validity of a scheme of four basic rhythms with two variant forms.

1	cretic + trochee or spondee	‾ ˘ ˘ ˘ , ‾ ˘ ‾ ‾	fórmă uérbŏrŭm
2	double cretic	‾ ˘ ‾ ‾ ˘ ˘	árte detérmĭnăt
3	cretic + double trochee or trochee + spondee	‾ ˘ ‾ ˘ ‾ ˘ ˘ / ‾ ˘ ‾ ˘ ‾ ‾	núptĭăs cŏnpárăbăt
4	cretic + iambus	‾ ˘ ‾ ˘ ˘	ánte díxĭmŭs
5	resolved cretic + trochee or spondee	‾ ˘ ˘ ˘ ˘ ˘ / ‾ ˘ ˘ ˘ ˘ ˘	ésse púĕrĭlĕ
6	resolved cretic + cretic	‾ ˘ ˘ ˘ ˘ ˘ ˘	ésse púĕrĭlĭtĕr

The fifth and sixth forms are simply variants of the first and second in which the last long syllable of the cretic is resolved into two short syllables. In all forms the first cretic may be strengthened to a molossus (‾ ‾ ‾). In all forms the last syllable is common. In the first two forms the first syllable of the cretic may be resolved. The third form appears sometimes only as a trochaic metron without the cretic, sometimes with a preceding trochee.

The form of the cursus widely taught in the Middle Ages as part of the *ars dictaminis* required stressed rhythms which can be perceived as reflexes of these quantitative rhythms.

1	planus	/ × × / ×	tráctibus trúdit
2	tardus	/ × × / × ×	fídens pernícibus

3	uelox	/ × × \ × / ×	agmínibus cìrcumsaéptus
4	medius	/ × / × ×	exercére stúdeat
5	trispondiacus	/ × × × / × *or* / × / × / ×	iaculórum catapúltas
6	dispondeus dactylicus	/ × × × / × ×	felíciter perfrúitur

EPISTOLA AD MILITES COROTICI

TEXT AND TRANSLATION

In the *Epistola* the four divisions marked Parts **I-IIII** are mine and putatively Patrick's. To the left in the first column, arabic numbers enclosed in round brackets represent the chapter divisions employed by all modern editors and commentators. The arabic numbers without brackets are my line numbers. Words *italicized* in the text and marked by lower case letters and lower case roman numerals ai–ii–bi–ii–b'i–ii–a'i–ii in the third column show parallel and chiastic connections within the separate parts **I-II-III-IIII**. Words underlined in the text and marked by upper case letters A1-2-3-B-C in the second column show connections between the larger divisions of the *Epistola*, between Parts **I** and **III** and between Parts **II** and **IIII** (note: the dotted line is broken at points where it would otherwise collide with descenders). Words in SMALL CAPITALS in the text but not marked to the left will be discussed in the analysis.

Letters and punctuation marks in boldface represent features of the manuscripts. Not all of these can be found in any single manuscript, but all of them can be found in at least one manuscript. The systems of disposing capital letters and punctuation marks are not identical any more than the systems of orthography and the textual readings are identical. But comparison of all the witnesses not only helps us to recover Patrick's original text; it proves beyond question that mediaeval readers apprehended Patrick's thought in something very like the units represented here. Some of the apparent oddities of punctuation issue from reversal of word order, which will be apparent to anyone who consults the manuscripts. Here it has seemed better to represent all the evidence than to appear to select only the favourable.

PART I

(1) A	1	a	**PATRICIUS** PECCATOR . *INDOCTUS* scilicet . *Hiberione*

(1) A 1 a **PATRICIUS** PECCATOR . *INDOCTUS* scilicet . *Hiberione*
        constitutus episcopum mé esse fáteor .

    2   Certissime reor *a DEO* 'accepi . id quod sum'.

    3   Inter barbaras itaque géntes hábito
        proselitus . et profuga ób amórem DÉI .

5   testis est ílle **si** íta est .
        Non quod optabam tam dure et tam aspere aliquid ex ore
        méo effúndere .

      bc   sed *cogor zelo DEI* ET UERITAS *XPÍSTI* . EXCITÁUIT .

      d   *pro dilectione proximorum átque filiórum*

    4   pro quibus 'tradidi' patriam et parentes et 'animam meam
        usque ad mortem' .

10   5 6 ef   Si dignus sum uiuo *DEO* méo *DOCÈRE* géntes .

    7   etsi contémpnor alíquibus .

(2)   g   Manu mea scripsi atque cóndidi *uèrba ísta*

  B   h   danda . et tradenda *militibus mitténda* . *COROTÍCI* .

    j   Non dico *ciuibus meis* . neque *ciuibus sanctórum Romanórum* .

15   k   sed ciuibus daemoniorum *ob mala ópera ipsórum*

    l   *Ritu hostíli . in mòrte uíuunt* .

  C   *Socii Scottorum . atque Pictorum apóstatarúmque* .

  D   k'   *sanguilentos sanguinare de sanguine innocentium Xpístianórum* .

  E   'quos' ego innumerum numerum DEO 'genui' . atque 'in
        Xpísto' confirmáui .

(3) F   j'   **P**ostera die qua *crismati neophyti* in uéste cándida

    h'   flagrabat in fronte ipsorum dum crudeliter trucidati atque
        mactati gládio . *sùpradíctis* .

    h'g'   *misi epistolam* cum sáncto presbýtero

    f'   quem ego ex infantia *DÓCUI* cum Cléricis .
        ut nobis aliquid indulgerent de praeda . uel de captiuis
        baptizátis quos cepérunt .

25   cachinnos fecérunt . de íllis .

(4) G   1   **I**dcirco nescio quid mágis lúgeam

    2   a   **a**n qui interfécti uel quòs cepérunt .

      b   uel quos grauiter zabulus ínlaqueáuit .
        Perenni poena gehennam pariter cum ípso mancipábunt .

30   **Q**uia utique 'qui facit peccatum seruus est' .
    et 'filius zábuli' nùncupátur .

(5)   3   e'   **Q**uapropter resciat omnis hómo timens *DÉUM*

    d'   *quod a mé aliéni sunt*

PART I

I, Patrick, a sinner, untaught, to be sure, established in Ireland, profess
    myself to be a bishop.
Most certainly I consider that I have received from God that which I am.
Consequently I dwell among barbarian gentiles
as a sojourner and a refugee because of the love of God.
He is the testifier whether that is so.
Not that I preferred to pour out from my mouth anything so harshly and
    so savagely,
but I am compelled by the zeal of God, and the truth of Christ has roused
    [me] up
for the love of [my] nearest neighbours and sons,
for whom I have handed over my fatherland and parents and my soul up to
    the point of death.
If I am worthy I live for my God to teach gentiles,
even if I am despised by some.
With my own hand I have written and composed these words,
to be given and handed over, dispatched to the soldiers of Coroticus,
I do not say to my fellow citizens, nor to fellow citizens of the holy Romans,
but to fellow citizens of demons because of their evil works.
By hostile behaviour they live in death,
comrades of Scots and Picts and apostates,
bloody men who are bloody with the blood of innocent Christians,
whom I have begotten for God, an innumerable number, and confirmed
    in Christ.
On the day after that on which the new converts in white clothing were
    anointed with chrism,
it was shining on their brow while they were relentlessly slaughtered and
    slain with the sword by the abovesaid men,
I dispatched an epistle with a holy presbyter,
whom I have taught from infancy, with clerics,
so that they might concede something to us from the loot or from the
    baptized captives whom they captured.
They made guffaws about them.
Because of that I do not know what I should lament more,
whether those who were killed, or those whom they captured,
or those whom the devil has oppressively ensnared.
In everlasting punishment they will subject [themselves] to hell equally
    with him,
because indeed he who commits sin is a slave,
and he is named a son of the devil.
On which account let every man fearing God get to know
that they are estranged from me

	c'b'	et a XPÍSTO DEO MÉO
35		*'pro quo legationem fungor'* .
		patricida . fratricida .'LUPI RAPACES deuorantes plebem DOMINI ut cibum panis'
H		sicut ait . 'Iniqui dissipauerunt LEGEM tuam DOMINE' .
J	a'	Quam in supremis temporibus *Hiberione* optime benígne *plantáuerat* .
39K		atque INSTRUCTA ÉRAT *fauènte* DÉO .

PART II

(6)		Non usurpo .
L		Pártem hábeo .
	a	cum hís *'quos aduocáuit et praedestinauit'* euangélium *praèdicáre* in persecutiónibus non *páruis* .
45		*'usque ad extremum terrae'* .
	b	Etsi inuidet inimicus per tyránnidem CÒROTÍCI . *qui Deum* non ueretur nec sacerdótes ipsíus
	c	quos elegit . et indulsit illis summam . diuinam . sublímam potestátem . *'quos ligarent super terram ligatos esse et in caelis'.*
(7)M N		UNDE ERGO quaeso plurimum 'sancti et humiles corde' adulari tálibus nón licet .
		'nec cibum' nec potum 'súmere' cum ípsis . nec elemosinas ipsorum récipi débeat . donec crudeliter paenitentiam effusis lacrimis satis Déo fáciant .
55O	d	et liberent seruos Dei et ancillas *Xpísti* baptizátas .
	e	pro quibus *mortuus ést* et crucifixus .
(8)		'Dona iniquorum reprobat Altissimus' . 'Qui offert sacrificium ex substantia pauperum . quasi qui uictimat filium in conspectu patris sui .'
60	f	*'Diuitias'* inquit *'quas congregauit iniuste* . euomentur de uentre eius .
	g	Trahit illum angelus mortis .
	h	Ira draconum mulcabitur .
	h'	INTERFICIET illum lingua colubris .
	g'	Comedit autem eum ignis inextinguibilis'.
65	f'	Ideoque 'Uae qui replent se quae non sunt sua'.

Uel 'Quid prodest homini ut totum mundum lucretur .

and from Christ my God,

for whom I perform an embassy.

Parricide, fratricide, rapacious wolves devouring the folk of the Lord as a meal [lit. 'food'] of bread.

Just as it declares, The unjust have utterly destroyed Your Law, Lord,

which in these last times He had propagated in Ireland most excellently, kindly,

and it had been built up [also 'instructed, taught'] with God favouring it.

PART II

I am not claiming too much.

I have a part

with those whom He has called to [Him]

and predestined to proclaim the Gospel

among not insignificant persecutions

as far as the most remote part of land,

even if the enemy shows his jealousy through the tyranny of Coroticus,

who is not in awe of God nor His priests,

whom He has chosen and conceded to them the highest divine sublime power,

that those whom they may bind on land are bound also in the heavens.

Whence therefore I request most of all, [you] holy and lowly in heart,

that it not be permitted to flatter such men,

to take neither food nor drink with them,

nor should one be obliged for alms of those men to be received

until they perform penance relentlessly enough with tears poured out to God

and free the slaves of God and the baptized handmaids of Christ,

for whom He died and was crucified.

The Most High reproves the gifts of unjust men.

He who offers sacrifice from the substance of poor men

[is] as he who makes a victim of a son in the sight of his own father.

The riches, it affirms, which he has gathered unrighteously will be vomited out from his belly.

The angel of death drags him away.

By the wrath of dragons he will be mutilated.

The tongue of the serpent will kill him.

Inextinguishable fire, moreover, eats him up.

And therefore, Woe to those who refill themselves with things which are not their own,

or, What advantage comes to a man that he should acquire as profit the whole world et animae suae detrimentum patiatur **?**'

(9)   Longum est per singula discutere . uel ínsinuáre

per totam legem carpere testimonia . de táli cupìditáte .

70   Auaritia . mortále crímen .

'Non concupisces rem proximi tui'.

e'   'Non *occides* .'

d'   Homicida non potest ésse cum *Xpísto* .

c'   'Qui odit fratrem suum . homicída .' *adscríbitur* .

75   Uel 'Qui non diligit fratrem suum in morte manet'.

b'   Quanto mágis *réus est* .

qui manus suas coinquinauit in sanguine filiórum *Déi* .

a'   *quos nuper 'adquisiuit' in ultimis terrae* . per *exhortationem*
        páruitátis nóstrae .

PART III

(10)A' 1 ab   Numquid sine *Deo uel* 'secundum carnem' . *Híberiòne*
        uéni **?**

80 2   Quís me cómpulit .

'Alligatus' sum 'Spiritu' . ut non uideam aliquem 'de
        cognatione mea' **?**

3   Numquid a me piam misericordiam quod ago érga
        gentem íllam

qui me aliquándo cepérunt .

4   et deuastauerunt seruos et ancillas dómus patris méi **?**

85 5   Ingenuus fui 'secundum carnem'

decurióne patre náscor .

Uendidi enim nobílitátem méam .

non erubesco néque me paénitet

pro utilitáte aliórum .

90 6   Denique seruus sum in Xpisto génti éxterae .

ob gloriam ineffabilem 'perennis uitae .

quae est in Xpisto Iesu Domino nostro'.

(11) 7   Et si mei mé non cognóscunt .

'propheta in patria sua honorem non habet'.

95   ci   *Forte non sumus 'ex uno ouili'* .

ii   *neque 'unum Deum pátrem' habémus* .

sicut ait . 'Qui non est mecum . contra me est .

et qui non congregat mecum . spargit'.

Non conuenit .

100   'Unus destruit .

alter aedificat .'

and suffer the loss of his own soul?

It is long-winded to shake out or make known from single cases,

to pluck from the whole Law testimonials about such greed.

Avarice [is] a mortal crime.

You shall not covet the possession of your neighbour.

You shall not murder.

A homicide cannot be with Christ.

He who hates his own brother is ascribed [or 'assigned to the category of']
   a homicide,

or, He who does not love dearly his own brother remains in death.

How much more guilty is he

who has defiled his own hands in the blood of the sons of God,

whom He has recently acquired in the furthest parts of land through the
   exhortation of our insignificance.

PART III

Can it be that I came to Ireland without God or according to the flesh?

Who compelled me?

I am bound by the Spirit that I should not see anyone from my kindred.

Can it be from myself that I perform a pious act of pity toward that gentile
   people

who once captured me

and ravaged the slaves and handmaids of my father's house?

I was freeborn according to the flesh.

I am born of a decurion father.

But I have sold my nobility,

I do not blush nor does it cause me regret,

for the advantage of others.

At the last I am a slave in Christ for that remote gentile people

because of the unutterable glory of everlasting life

which is in Christ Jesus our Lord.

If even mine do not recognize me,

a prophet does not have honour in his own fatherland.

Perhaps we are not from one sheepfold,

and we do not have one God as father.

Just as He declares, He who is not with me is against me,

and he who does not gather with me scatters.

It does not come together:

One destroys;

another builds.

'**N**on quaero quae mea sunt .'
Non méa grátia .
sed Deus 'qui dedit hanc sollicitudinem in corde meo' .
105   ut unus essem de 'uenatoribus siue piscatoribus'
quos olim Deus 'in nouissimis diebus' ánte praenùntiáuit .
(12)   Ínuidetur míhi .

di   *Q*uid *fáciam Dómine* ?
ii   *Uálde despícior* .
110   iii   *Ecce oues tuae circa me laniantur átque depraedántur* .
B'   et supradictis latrunculis iubente COROTÍCO hostìli .
                ménte .
    iv ei   *Longe est a caritate Dei traditor Xpístianórum*
C'   ii   *in manus* Scottorum átque *Pictórum*
         'LUPI RAPACES' DEGLUTIERUNT GRÉGEM DÓMINI .
115   qui utique Hiberione cum summa diligentia óptime
           crescébat .
D'   iii   *Et filii Scottorum et filiae règulórum* .
         monachi et uírgines Xpísti .
E'   iv   *enumeráre néqueo* .

f   *Q*uam ob rem 'iniuria IUSTORUM non te placeat'.
120   etiam 'usque ad inferos non placebit'.
(13)   *Q*uis sanctorum non hórreat iòcundáre .
    uel conuiuium frúere . cum tálibus
g   *D*e spoliis *defunctorum* Xpistianorum repleuérunt domos
        súas ?
    *D*é rapínis uíuunt .
125   h   *N*esciunt miseri uenenum . letale cibum porrigunt ad
        amicos et fílios súos .
   ji   sicut Eua non intellexit quod utique mortem . *trádidit*
        uìro súo .
   ii   *Sic sunt ómnes qui màle águnt*
   iii   *'mortem' perennem poénam 'operántur'.*
(14)   k   *C*onsuetudo *Romanorum* Gallorum *Xpístianórum*
130   mittunt uiros sanctos idoneos *ad Francos* . *et céteras géntes* .
    cum tot milia solidorum . *ad redimendos captíuos baptizátos* .
   k'   *T*U potius INTERFICIS et *uendis illos genti exterae* ígnoranti
        Déum .
   j'i   quasi in LUPANAR *trádis* 'membra Xpísti'.

    *Q*ualem spem hábes in Déum .
135   uel quí te conséntit .
    aut qui te communicat uerbis ádulatiónis .
    Déus iudicábit ?
   ii   **S**criptum est enim . '*N*on solum facientes mala .

I do not seek the things which are mine.
Not by my grace,
but God Who has given this solicitude in my heart,
so that I should be one of the hunters or fishers
whom God foretold once before for the final days.
Jealousy is shown to me.
What shall I do, Lord?
I am especially despised.
Look, Your sheep are torn to pieces around me and looted,
even by the abovesaid wretched little thieves, with Coroticus commanding
    from his hostile mind.
Far off from the charity of God is the betrayer of Christians
into the hands of Scots and Picts.
Rapacious wolves have gulped down the flock of the Lord,
which was indeed growing most excellently in Ireland with the highest
    loving care.
Both sons and daughters of the petty kings of the Scots
[were] monks and virgins of Christ,
I cannot count out.
For which reason may the injustice done to the righteous not please You,
even as far as the lower depths it will not please.
Which of the holy ones would not be horrified to rejoice
or to enjoy a banquet with such men?
From the spoils of deceased Christians they have refilled their houses.

They live from plunderings.
They do not know, pitiable men, that they offer poison, a lethal food to
    their own friends and sons,
just as Eve did not understand that she certainly handed over death to her
    own husband.
So are all who perform badly;
they work death as an everlasting punishment.
The custom of the Christian Roman Gauls:
they dispatch holy substantial men to the Franks and other gentiles
with so many thousands of solidi for redeeming baptized captives;
you rather kill and sell them to a remote gentile people ignorant of God,

as if you are handing over into a brothel [lit. 'house of she-wolves'] the
    members of Christ.
What hope do you have in God,
or anyone who agrees with you,
or who communicates with you in words of flattery?
God will judge.
For it is written, Not only those committing bad deeds,

	iii		*sed etiam consentientes damnandi sunt .'*
(15)		h'	**N**éscio 'quid dícam'
			uel 'quid lóquar' ámplius
F'		g'	de defunctis
		f'i*a*	*filiórum Déi .*
		b	*quos gladius supra modum dúre tétigit .*
145		ii	**S**criptum est enim . *'Flete cum flentibus .'*
		iii	**E**t iterum . *'Si dolet unum membrum .*
		iii'	*condoleant omnia membra'.*
G'	3	ii'	**Q**uapropter ecclesia *'plorat . et plangit*
		i'*a*	*filios' et filias 'súas'*
150	2	a *b*	*quas adhuc gladius nóndum interfécit .*
			Sed prolongati et exportati in lónga terrárum .
		b	ubi 'peccatum' manifeste grauiter . impudénter 'abúndat'.
			Ibi uenundati ingénui hómines .
		e' i	*Xpistiani in seruitúte redácti sunt .*
155		ii	**P**raesertim indignissimorum . pessimorum apostatarúmque
			. *Pictórum* .
(16)	1		**I**dcirco cum tristitia et maerore uóciferábo .
		iii	**O** speciosissimi atque *amantissimi fratres et filii 'quos in*
			Xpisto genui' .
		iv	*enumeráre néqueo .*
		d' i	**Q**uid fáciam uóbis **?**
160		ii	*Non sum dignus Deo neque homínibus sùbueníre .*
H'		iii	*'Praeualuit iniquitas iniquorum super nos .'*
		iv	*Quasi 'extranei facti sumus'.*
		c' i	*Forte non credunt . 'Unum báptismum' percépimus .*
		ii	*uel 'unum Deum pátrem' habémus .*
J'		b'	**I**ndignum est illis *Hibérionàci* súmus
K'			**S**icut ait . 'Nonne unum *Deum* habetis **?**'
167			'Quid dereliquistis unusquisque proximum suum **?**'

PART **IIII**

(17)	**I**dcirco dóleo pro uóbis .
	doleo caríssimi míhi .
170	sed iterum . gaudeo íntra meípsum .
	non grátis 'laboráui' .
	uel peregrinatio mea 'in uácuum' nón fuit .
	Et contigit scelus tam horréndum ineffábile .
a	**D**eo gratias . créduli *bàptizáti* .
175	DE SAECULO RECESSÍSTIS AD PÀRADÍSUM .
	Cerno uos .

but also those agreeing with [them] are to be condemned.
I do not know what I shall say
or what I shall speak further
about the deceased
of the sons of God
whom the sword has touched harshly beyond measure.
For it is written, Weep with those weeping,
and again, If one member grieves
all members should grieve together.
On which account the Church cries and bewails
its own sons and daughters
whom so far the sword has not yet killed,
but removed afar and deported to far-off places of lands
where sin openly, oppressively, impudently abounds;
there freeborn men are given for sale;
Christians are reduced to slavery,
particularly among the most unworthy worst apostates and Picts.

Because of that I shall raise my voice with sadness and mourning.
O most beautiful and most beloved brothers and sons whom I have
    begotten in Christ,
I cannot count out,
what shall I do for you?
I am not worthy to come to the support of God nor men.
The injustice of unjust men has prevailed over us,
as if we have been made remote outsiders.
Perhaps they do not believe we have received one baptism
or we have one God as father.
It is scandalous [lit. 'unworthy'] to them that we are Irish.
Just as it declares, Do you not have one God?
Why have you abandoned, each one of you, his own neighbour?

PART IIII

Because of that I grieve for you,
I grieve, dearest to me,
but again I rejoice within myself.
Not for free have I laboured,
or my exile has not been in vain.
And the shameful deed, so horrendous, unutterable, has befallen so that,
thanks be to God, as baptized faithful men
you have departed from this age to paradise.
I perceive you clearly,

migrare coepistis **u**bi 'nox non erit'. 'neque luctus .
    neque mors . amplius' .
'sed exultabitis sicut uituli ex uinculis resoluti .
et conculcabitis iniquos .

180   et erunt cinis sub pedibus uestris'.

(18)   b   UOS ERGO REGNABITIS cum *apostolis . et prophetis . átque*
                martýribus .
               A ETERNA RÉGNA . CAPIÉTIS .

        ci   *sicut ípse testátur .*

        ii   *Inquit .*

185   d   '*Uenient ab oriente . et occidente .*
               et recumbent . cum Abraham . et Isaac . et Iacob . IN REGNO
                 CAELORUM'.

        e   '*Foris canes . et uenefici . et homicidae' .*

L'   et '*Mendacibus . periuris . pars eorum . IN STAGNUM IGNIS*
                 AETERNI' .

        f   **N**on inmerito ait apostolus . '*Ubi IUSTUS uix saluus erit .*

190   *PECCATOR . et impius transgressor LEGIS ubi se recognoscet* **?**'

(19)M'   f'   UNDE ENIM COROTICUS . *cum suis scéleratíssimis*
               rebellatores Xpisti úbi se uidébunt .
               Qui mulierculas baptizatas . praémia distríbuunt .
               Ob MISERUM RÉGNUM TEMPORÁLE .

195   quod utique in moménto tránseat .

        e'   '*Sicut . nubes . uel fumus . qui utique uento dispergitur' .*
               ita '*peccatores' fraudulenti . 'a facie Domini peribunt .*

        d'   **I**usti *autem epulentur in magna constántia' cum Xpísto .*
               '*iudicabunt nationes . ET' REGIBUS INIQUIS 'DOMINABUNTUR' .*

200   IN SAÉCULA SAÈCULÓRUM . AMEN .

(20)   c'i   'TESTIFICOR CORAM DEO *et* angelis *suis' . quod ita erit .*
               sicut intimauit imperítiae méae .

        ii   **N**ón *mea uérba .*

        b'   *sed Dei . et apostolorum átque prophetárum .*
               quod ego Latínum expósui .

205   **Q**ui numquam énim mentíti sunt .
               'Qui crediderit . saluus erit .
               qui uero non crediderit . condempnabitur .
               Deus locutus est' .

(21)N'   **Q**uaeso plurimum . ut quicumque famulus . Dei .
               prómptus fúerit .

210   ut sit gerulus lítterárum hárum .
              ut nequáquam subtrahátur .
              uel abscondátur a némine .

you have begun to journey where there will not be night nor lament nor
   death any more,
but you will exult just as calves freed from chains,
and you will trample down the unjust underfoot,
and they will be dust under your feet.
You therefore will reign with apostles and prophets and martyrs,

you will capture eternal realms.
Just as He Himself testifies,
He affirms,
They will come from the rising and the setting [*i.e.* from east and west],
and they will lie back with Abraham and Isaac and Jacob in the realm of
   the heavens.
Outside dogs and makers of poison and homicides,
and their portion with lying perjurers in the pool of eternal fire.

Not undeservedly the apostle declares, Where the righteous man will
   scarcely be saved,
where will the sinner and impious transgressor of the Law recognize
   himself?
Whence, then, Coroticus with his most shameful men,
rebels against Christ, where will they see themselves,
they who distribute baptized little women as prizes
because of a pitiable temporal realm
which may indeed pass away in a moment?
Just as a cloud or smoke, which indeed is dispersed by the wind,
so fraudulent sinners will perish from the face of the Lord.
But the righteous will feast in great constancy with Christ.
They will judge nations, and they will lord it over unjust rulers
for ages of ages. Amen.
I bear testimony before God and His angels that it will be so, just as He
   has intimated to my unlearnedness.
Not my words,
but God's and the apostles' and prophets',
which I have set out in Latin,
who, however, have never lied.
He who will have believed will be saved,
but he who will not have believed will be condemned.
God has spoken.
I request most of all that any servant of God will have been quick to
   respond,
that he may be bearer of this letter,
that it by no means be stolen,
or that it be hidden by no one,

sed magis potius legatur coram cúnctis plébibus .
et praesente ípso CoROTÍCO .

215   Quod si Deus inspirat illos 'ut quandoque Deo resipiscant'.

Ita ut uel sero paeniteant . quod tam ímpie gessérunt .
Homicida erga frátres Dómini .

N'   a'   et liberent captiuas *baptizatas* quas ánte cepérunt .
ita ut mereantur Déo uíuere .

220   et sáni efficiántur .
híc et in aetérnum .
PAX PATRI . ET FILIO . ET SPIRÍTUI SÁNCTO . *AMEN* —:

but much rather that it be read before all folk,
even Coroticus himself being present.
Which if God inspires them that whenever they return to their senses for
    God,
or so that they may repent [even] late what they have done so impiously,
homicide against the brothers of the Lord,
and they may free baptized captive women whom they captured before,
so that they may deserve to live for God
and be made sane
here and for eternity.
Peace to the Father and to the Son and to the Holy Spirit. Amen.

EPISTOLA AD MILITES
COROTICI

ANALYSIS AND COMMENTARY

The first aspect of structure to note is the antiphonally paired statements, with which Patrick imitated the style of the Latin Bible. By attending to the meaning and structure of these short units reader and hearer alike discover both the order of Patrick's thought and the rhythm of his prose. Of the lines which contain at least five syllables and which do not end entirely in Biblical quotation, one exhibits the stressed reflex of the trochaic metron ¯ ˇ ¯ ˇ *mortále crímen* 70, and six (five with one repeated, lines 4, 77, 87, 124, 143, 210) exhibit the rhythm /×/×/×. All of those seven, 3.15% of the total number of lines in the *Epistola*, would conform to other more acceptable cursus types after reversal of the order of the last words, but the present order of words is fixed by devices which we shall consider shortly.

The second aspect of structure to note is the four paragraphs, the limits of each of which are established by internal chiasmus.

In part **I** compare the beginning a *indoctus ... Hiberione constitutus ... a Deo* in lines 1-2 with the end a' *Hiberione ... plantauerat ... instructa erat fauente Deo* in lines 38-9; b *cogor zelo Dei* 7 with b' *Deo meo pro quo legationem fungor* 34-5; c *Xpisti* 7 with c' *Xpisto* 34; d 'neighbours and sons' 8 with d' 'aliens' 33; e *Deo* 10 with e' *Deo* 34; f *docere* 10 with f' *docui* 23; the reference to Patrick's letter in g *uerba ista* 12 with that in g' *epistolam* 22; h *militibus mittenda Corotici* 13 with h' *supradictis misi* 21-2; Patrick's fellow citizens in j *ciuibus meis ... ciuibus sanctorum Romanorum* 14 with those who joined them through baptism in j' *crismati neophyti* 20; evil men and their deeds in k *ob mala opera ipsorum* 15 with those in k' *sanguilentos sanguinare de sanguine innocentium Xpistianorum* 18. At the crux of the chiasmus in l Patrick attacks their bad behaviour and names their accomplices 16-7.

In part **II** compare a *quos aduocauit et praedestinauit ... praedicare ... paruis ... ad extremum terrae* 42-5 with a' *quos nuper adquisiuit in ultimis terrae ... exhortationem paruitatis* 78; b *Corotici qui Deum* 46-7 with b' *reus est* [*i.e.* *Coroticus*] *qui ... Dei* 76-7; c the priestly power to bind 48-9 with c' ascription to a legal and moral category 74; d *Xpisti* 55 with d' *Xpisto* 73; e *mortuus est* 56 with e' *occides* 72; f *diuitias inquit quas congregauit iniuste* 60 with f' *ideoque uae qui replent se quae non sunt sua* 65; g *trahit illum angelus mortis* 61 with g' *comedit autem eum ignis inextinguibilis* 64; h *ira draconum mulcabitur* 62 with h' *interficiet illum lingua colubris* 63.

In part **III** compare a *Deo* 79 with a' *Deum* 166; b *Hiberione* 79 with b' *Hiberionaci* 165; ci *forte non sumus ex uno ouili* 95 with c'i *forte non credunt unum baptismum percepimus* 163; cii *neque unum Deum patrem habemus* 96 with c'ii *uel unum Deum patrem habemus* 164; di *quid faciam, Domine* 108 with d'i *quid faciam uobis* 159; dii *ualde despicior* 109 with d'ii *non sum dignus Deo neque hominibus subuenire* 160; diii *ecce oues tuae circa me laniantur atque depraedantur* 110 with d'iii *praeualuit iniquitas iniquorum super nos* 161; div *longe est a caritate Dei* 112 with d'iv *quasi extranei facti sumus* 162; ei *traditor Xpistianorum in manus* 112-3 with e'i *Xpistiani in seruitute redacti sunt* 154; eii *Pictorum* 113 with e'ii *Pictorum* 155; eiii *et filii Scottorum et filiae regulorum monachi et uirgines Xpisti* 116-7 with e'iii *amantissimi fratres et filii quos in Xpisto genui* 157; eiv *enumerare nequeo* 118 with e'iv *enumerare nequeo* 158; compare f *iniuria iustorum non te placeat, etiam usque ad inferos non placebit* 119-20, a Biblical quotation from Ecclesiasticus IX 17 introduced by *quam ob rem*, with its pair f' 143-50 exhibiting internal chiasmus: ia *filiorum Dei* balanced by i'a *filios et filias suas*; ib *quos gladius supra modum dure tetigit* by i'b *quas adhuc gladius nondum interfecit*; ii *flete cum flentibus* by ii' *plorat et plangit*; iii *si dolet unum membrum* by iii' *condoleant omnia membra*, a Biblical quotation from Matthew II 18 introduced by *quapropter*. Compare g *de ... defunctorum* 123 with g' *de defunctis* 142; h *nesciunt* 125 with h' *nescio* 140; ji *tradidit* 126 with j'i *tradis* 133; jii *sic sunt omnes qui male agunt* 127 with j'ii *non solum facientes mala* 138; jiii *mortem perennem poenam operantur* 128 with j'iii *sed etiam consentientes damnandi sunt* 139. At the crux of the chiasmus in kk' Patrick contrasts the behaviour of the Roman Christian Gauls, who redeem captive Christians from pagans 129-31, with that of the Roman Christian Briton Coroticus, identified here only as *Tu*, who sells captive Christians to pagans 132-3.

In part **IIII** compare a *baptizati* 174 with a' *baptizatas* 218; b *apostolis et prophetis atque* 181 with b' *et apostolorum atque prophetarum* 203; ci *ipse* [*sc.Deus*] *testatur* 183 with c'i *testificor* [*sc. Patricius*] *coram Deo* 201; cii *inquit* [*sc. Deus*] 184 with c'ii *non mea uerba* [*sc. Patricii*] *sed Dei* 202-3; d *uenient ab oriente et occidente et recumbent cum Abraham et Isaac et Iacob in regno caelorum* 185-6 with d' *iusti autem epulentur in magna constantia cum Xpisto, iudicabunt nationes et regibus iniquis dominabuntur* 198-9; compare the banishment and punishment of the wicked in e 187-8 with that in e' 196-7; and the rhetorical questions at the crux in f 189-90 and f' 191-5.

These internal chiastic and parallel patterns fix both the outer limits and the chiastic crux of each of the paragraphs. But these patterns comprise only part of Patrick's comprehensive ordering of his thought and prose. He linked part **I** to part **III** and part **II** to part **IIII** with a series of parallels.

Considering links between parts **I** and **III** compare A1 *Hiberione constitutus* 1 with A'1 *Hiberione ueni* 79; A2 *a Deo accepi id quod sum* 2 with A'2 *Quis me compulit? Alligatus sum Spiritu* 80-1; A3 *inter barbaras itaque gentes habito* 3 with A'3 *ago erga gentem illam qui me aliquando ceperunt et deuastauerunt seruos et ancillas domus* 82-4; A4 *parentes* 9 with A'4 *patris mei*

84; A5 *si dignus sum* 10 with A'5 *ingenuus fui secundum carnem, decurione patre nascor, uendidi enim nobilitatem meam* 85-7; A6 *gentes* 10 with A'6 *genti exterae* 90; A7 *etsi contempnor aliquibus* 11 with A'7 *et si mei me non cognoscunt* 93. Compare B *militibus* ... *Corotici* 13 with B' *supradictis latrunculis iubente Corotico* 111; C *Scottorum atque Pictorum* 17 with C' *Scottorum atque Pictorum* 113; D *innocentium Xpistianorum* 18 with D' *et filii Scottorum et filiae regulorum monachi et uirgines Xpisti* 116-7; E *quos ego innumerum numerum Deo genui atque in Xpisto confirmaui* 19 with E' *enumerare nequeo* 118 and *quos in Xpisto genui enumerare nequeo* 157-8; F *crismati neophyti* ... *trucidati atque mactati gladio* 20-1 with F' *de defunctis filiorum Dei quos gladius supra modum dure tetigit* 142-4; G1 *idcirco nescio quid magis lugeam* 26 with G'1 *idcirco cum tristitia et maerore uociferabo* 156; G2a *interfecti* 27 with G'2a *interfecit* 150; G2b *grauiter* 28 with G'2b *grauiter* 152; G3 *quapropter* 32 with G'3 *quapropter* 148; H *iniqui* 37 with H' *iniquitas iniquorum* 161; J *Hiberione* 38 with J' *Hiberionaci* 165; and K *Deo* 39 with K' *Deum* 166.

These parallels are not only clear; they extend to the letter K, as the internal chiastic and parallel elements of both parts **I** and **III** extend to the letters k and l. And there are many more links between parts **I** and **III** which do not occur in parallel order. Compare *proximorum* 8 with *proximum* 167, *patriam* 9 with *patria* 94, *mittenda* 13 with *mittunt* 130, *dico* 14 with *dicam* 140, *sanctorum* 14 with *sanctorum* 121, *Romanorum* 14 with *Romanorum* 129, *hostili* 16 with *hostili* 111, *uiuunt* 16 with *uiuunt* 124, *perenni poena* 29 with *perennem poenam* 128, *peccatum* 30 with *peccatum* 152, *seruus* 30 with *seruus* 90, *timens Deum* 32 with *ignoranti Deum* 132, *sicut ait* 37 with *sicut ait* 97, 166, *quam in supremis temporibus* ... *plantauerat* 38 with *quos* ... *Deus in nouissimis diebus* ... *praenuntiauit* 106, and *optime* 38 with *optime* 115.

Considering links in parallel order between parts **II** and **IIII** compare L *partem* 41 with L' *pars* 188, M *unde ergo* 50 with M' *unde enim* 191, N *quaeso plurimum* 50 with N' *quaeso plurimum* 209, and O *et liberent* ... *baptizatas* 55 with O' *et liberent* ... *baptizatas* 218. There are more links between parts **II** and **IIII** which do not occur in parallel order. Compare *iniquorum* 57 with *iniquis* 199, *inquit* 60 with *inquit* 184, *angelus* 61 with *angelis* 201, *ignis inextinguibilis* 64 with *in stagnum ignis aeterni* 188, and *homicida non potest esse cum Xpisto* 73 with *foris canes et uenefici et homicidae* 187.

Patrick further linked parts **I** and **II** and parts **III** and **IIII**. The clearest indications of this are that parts **I** and **II** both begin similarly with professions of authority, *episcopum me esse fateor* 1 and *partem habeo cum his quos aduocauit et praedestinauit euangelium praedicare* 41-3, and both end similarly with accounts of his evangelization, *legem* ... *quam in supremis temporibus Hiberione optime benigne plantauerat atque instructa erat fauente Deo* 38-9 and *[filios] quos nuper adquisiuit in ultimis terrae per exhortationem paruitatis nostrae* 78. Also the word *iustorum* occurs in part **III** f at line 119 and *iustus* in part **IIII** f at line 189. For links between parts **I** and **II** compare *testis* 5 with *testimonia* 69, *effundere* 6 with *effusis* 54, *proximorum* 8 with *proximi* 71, *pro quibus … ad mortem* 9 with *pro quibus mortuus est* 56, *animam* 9 with *animae* 67, *in morte uiuunt* 16 with *in morte manet* 75, *de sanguine innocentium Xpistianorum* 18 with *in sanguine filiorum Dei* 77, *crudeliter* 21 with *crudeliter* 54, *nobis … indulgerent* 24 with *indulsit illis* 48, and *legem* 37 with *legem* 69. For links between parts **III** and **IIII** compare *ueni* 79 with *uenient* 185, *ineffabilem* 91 with *ineffabile* 173, *propheta* 94 with *prophetis* 181 and *prophetarum* 203, *non mea gratia sed Deus* 103-4 with *non mea uerba sed Dei* 202-3, *iustorum* 119 with *iusti* 198, *miseri* 125 with *miserum* 194, *uenenum* 125 with *uenefici* 187, *loquar* 141 with *locutus est* 208, *amplius* 141 with *amplius* 177, *dolet … condoleant* 146-7 with *doleo … doleo* 168-9, *idcirco* 156 with *idcirco* 168, and *iniquorum* 161 with *iniquos* 179.

Patrick further linked parts **I** and **IIII** and parts **II** and **III**. The clearest indications of this are that the word *peccator* at the beginning of part **I** 1 recurs at the crux of part **IIII** f 190, the line after *iustus*, which links **IIII** f to **III** f, and the word *interficiet* in the second half of the crux of **II** 63 is echoed by *interficis* in the second half of the crux of **III** 132. For links between parts **I** and **IIII** compare *peccator* 1 with *peccator* 190 and *peccatores* 197, *si dignus sum uiuo Deo* 10 with *ita ut mereantur Deo uiuere* 219, *captiuis baptizatis quos ceperunt* 24 with *captiuas baptizatas quas ante ceperunt* 218, *idcirco* 26 with *idcirco* 168, *lugeam* 26 with *luctus* 177, *patricida fratricida* 36 with *homicida erga fratres* 217. For links between parts **II** and **III** compare *inuidet* 46 with *inuidetur* 107, *summam* 48 with *summa* 115, *adulari* 51 with *adulationis* 136, *talibus* 51 with *talibus* 122, *seruos … et ancillas* 55 with *seruos et ancillas* 84, *quasi* 59 with *quasi* 133, *congregauit* 60 with *congregat* 98, *interficiet* 63 with *interficis* 132, *replent* 65 with *repleuerunt* 123, *longum est* 68 with *longe est* 112 and *longa* 151, *manus* 77 with *manus* 113, *filiorum Dei* 77 with *filiorum Dei* 143.

Patrick has left a further indication of order in his *Epistola* by counting the lines. There are thirty-nine in part **I**, thirty-nine in part **II**, eighty-nine in part **III**, and fifty-five in part **IIII**, exactly 222, CCXXII, in the entire composition. The number of lines in part **I** is equalled by the number of lines in part **II**. The number of lines in part **III**, 89, added to that in part **IIII**, 55, totals 144, which divides by extreme and mean ratio at 89 and 55. One can be certain that the number of lines is correct by comparing the thirty-sixth line of part **I**, *lupi rapaces deuorantes plebem Domini*, with the thirty-sixth line of part **III**, *lupi rapaces deglutierunt gregem Domini*, and with lines 132-3, thirty-sixth from the end of part **III**, *tu potius interficis et uendis illos genti exterae ignoranti Deum quasi in lupanar tradis membra Xpisti*.

A final indication of the textual integrity of the *Epistola*, an indication which confirms all the others, is the counting of words and their disposition at arithmetically fixed intervals. There are four words in the title, 269 in part **I**, 230 in part **II**, 486 in part **III**, and 311 in part **IIII**, exactly 1300 in the entire composition.

In part **I** Patrick affirms his episcopal authority to teach, stating at the beginning that he is *indoctus* 1, at d that he lives *docere* 10, at d' that he dispatched with an epistle a presbyter whom he had taught, *docui* 23, and at the end that God's law *instructa erat* in Ireland 39. The 269 words of part **I** divide by extreme and mean ratio at 166 and 103, at *quem ego ex infantia* | *docui*.

In part **II** the symmetrical centre of the 230 words falls at the end of line 59 and the beginning of line 60 *diuitias inquit quas congregauit iniuste*, the chiastic passage of which the crux is the thematic centre of the chiasmus of the entire paragraph.

In part **III** the number of lines, 89, divides by extreme and mean ratio at 55 and 34, and the number of words, 486, at 300 and 186. The crux of the chiasmus is the passage in which Patrick contrasts the behaviour of Christian Roman Gauls with that of Coroticus:

> Consuetudo Romanorum Gallorum Xpistianorum
> mittunt uiros sanctos idoneos ad Francos et ceteras gentes
> cum tot milia solidorum ad redimendos captiuos baptizatos.
> Tu potius interficis et uendis illos genti exterae ignoranti Deum
> quasi in lupanar tradis membra Xpisti.

The passage is bound tightly with various structural links. The second sentence, beginning thirty-six lines from the end of the paragraph, is connected to the thirty-sixth line from the beginning of the paragraph by association of *lupanar* with *lupi rapaces*, which connects in turn with the thirty-sixth line of part **I**, *lupi rapaces*. The second sentence ends in line 133, at the golden section, the fifty-fifth line of the paragraph. The thirty-seven words of this passage divide by extreme and mean ratio at 23 and 14, at *tu potius* | *interficis*, exactly at the word which links the crux of part **III** to the crux of part **II** *interficiet* 63. The 486 words of part **III** divide by extreme and mean ratio at 300 and 186, at *ad redimendos* | *captiuos baptizatos*, which is followed directly by the contrasting *tu potius* | *interficis*.

In part **IIII** the number of lines, 55, divides by extreme and mean ratio at 34 and 21. The number of words, 311, divides by symmetry at 156 and by extreme and mean ratio at 192 and 119. The thirty-fourth line from the end of the paragraph is 189, the beginning of the crux of the chiasmus.

> Non inmerito ait apostolus 'Ubi iustus uix saluus erit
> peccator et impius transgressor legis ubi se recognoscet?
> Unde enim Coroticus cum suis sceleratissimis
> rebellatores Xpisti ubi se uidebunt
> qui mulierculas baptizatas praemia distribuunt
> ob miserum regnum temporale
> quod utique in momento transeat?

The following word *sicut* 196 is the central 156th word of the paragraph. The 119th word is *iustus*, which connects part **IIII** f with part **III** f *iustorum* in line 119 of the entire composition. The first word of line 190, *peccator*, echoes the beginning of part **I**, *Patricius peccator*, and the word *legis* in the same line echoes the end of part **I** *legem* 37. The first words of line 191 *unde enim* are among the parallels which link part **IIII** with part **II** *unde ergo* 50.

The thirty-fourth line from the beginning of part **IIII** begins *testificor coram Deo* and is followed, twenty-one lines later, by *Pax Patri et Filio et Spiritui Sancto Amen* 222. It is preceded by the thirty-third line of part **IIII**, the 200th of the entire composition, *in saecula saeculorum Amen*. From *de saeculo recessistis ad paradisum* 175 to *in saecula saeculorum Amen* 200 inclusive there are 156 words, half the words of part **IIII**. Exactly half way, seventy-eight words from the beginning and seventy-eight words from the end of this passage, Patrick tells where the wicked will go, *in stagnum ignis aeterni* in line 188, at the golden section of the lines of part **IIII**, 21. Those seventy-eight words divide by extreme and mean ratio at 41 and 30. After *de saeculo recessistis ad paradisum* 175 the thirtieth word is the first of *uos ergo regnabitis* 181, and from *uos* inclusive the thirtieth word is the first of *in regno caelorum* 186. After *de saeculo recessistis ad paradisum* the forty-first word is the last of *aeterna regna capietis* 182. The forty-first word before *in saecula saeculorum* is the first of *miserum regnum temporale* 194. After that the thirtieth word is the first of *et regibus iniquis dominabuntur* 199, which is followed directly by *in saecula saeculorum Amen*.

Patrick refers to God thirty-three times in the *Epistola*, thirty-two as *Deus*, and once at the very end as the Trinity. He refers to *Xpistus* twelve times, *Dominus* seven times, *Xpistiani* five times, *Hiberione* and *Hiberionaci* five times, *Scotti* and *Picti* three times each, *Romani* twice, and *Galli* once.

Note the disposition of the words *Deus*, *Xpistus*, and *Dominus* in part **I**. From the beginning of the *Epistola Deo* 2 is the fourteenth word (7×2), between which and *Dei* 4 there are fourteen words. After *Dei* 4 *Deo* 10 is the forty-ninth word (7×7), and between these the central words are *Dei et ueritas Xpisti excitauit* 7. From *Deo* 10 to *Deo* 19 inclusive there are fifty-six words (7×8). Between *Deo* 19 and *Deum* 32 there are ninety-one words (7×13). Between *Deum* 32 and *Xpisto Deo meo* 34 there are seven words (7×1). After *Deo* 34 *Deo* 39 is the thirty-fifth word (7×5) and the last word of part **I**. The twenty-fourth word before the end of part **I** is *Domini* 36. The golden section of 24 falls at 15 and 9. Between *Domini* 36 and *Domine* 37 there are nine words.

Note the disposition of the name *Coroticus*, which occurs once in the title and five times in the text of the *Epistola*, first as *Corotici* at the end of line 13, fifth and last as *Corotico* in line 214, the ninth line from the end. The first thirteen lines and the last nine lines together comprise twenty-two lines of a total of 222. The golden section of 22 falls at 13.6 and 8.4. The name occurs second as *Corotici* at the end of line 46, the thirty-third line after the first occurrence and the thirty-third line from the end of part **II**. It occurs third as *Corotico* in line 111, the thirty-third line line of part **III**. Patrick addresses the tyrant as *Tu* in line 132, the twenty-second line from line 111 inclusive. Between the fourth occurrence of the name as *Coroticus* in line 191 and the fifth as *Corotico* in line 214 there are twenty-two lines. The fifth and last occurrence is the fiftieth word from the end of the *Epistola*. Beginning at the title the hundredth word, *mittenda*, brings one to the first occurrence of the name in the text at line 13. From the second occurrence to the third inclusive there are 199 words. The text of the entire letter with title contains exactly 1300 words, which divide by epogdous, one-ninth and eight-ninths, at 144.44 and 1155.56. Before the first occurrence of the name *Corotici* in line 13 there are ninety-six words, and after the fifth and last occurrence of the name *Corotico* in line 214 there are forty-nine words, together 145 words. The title *Epistola ad Milites Corotici* contains four words and the text of the letter from the first mention of the name *Corotici* to the last mention of the name *Corotico* inclusive contains 1151 words, together 1155 words.

This is by no means an exhaustive analysis of the art of Patrick's *Epistola*. It merely scratches the surface. But it suggests what may lie in the depths of this remarkable letter.

CONFESSIO

OUTLINE OF THE STRUCTURE

In the following outline of the chiastic structure of the *Confessio*, Parts **I-V** marked in boldface are mine and putatively Patrick's. Arabic figures enclosed in round brackets (1-62) are the traditional chapter numbers used by all modern editors and commentators. Upper case roman numerals I-XXVI designate my division of the text into chapters, putatively Patrick's. Upper case letters A-N-A' represent the chiastic and parallel pairings of these chapters.

			Christ commanded him to stay in Ireland, echo of Psalm CXVIII 60, influence of the Holy Spirit
(44–45)		7	Devotion to duty in Ireland
(46)		6'	Former willingness to go to Ireland, echo of Psalm CXVIII 60, influence of the Holy Spirit
(47–49)		5'	*Fratres Xpistiani et uirgines Xpisti*
(49–51)		4'	Baptisms, ordinations, and confirmation of Faith in remote places
(50–53)		3'	What Patrick has given
(53)		2'	Echo of Romans XV 24
(53 end)		1'	*Meipsum impendam pro animabus uestris [Hiberionacum]*, echoing II Corinthians XII 5

PART V

(54)	XXI	F'	On truthfulness
(55)	XXII	E'	Confession of unworthiness
(55end–56)	XXIII	D'	Reliance upon God, quoting Psalm LIV 23
(57–60)	XXIIII	C'	Doxology, quoting Romans VIII 16-7
(61)	XXV	B'	Restatement of reason for writing, echoing Psalm CXVIII 111
(62)	XXVI	A'	Epilogue. Author's identification

CONFESSIO

TEXT AND TRANSLATION

In the following text of the *Confessio* letters and punctuation marks in bold-face represent features of the manuscripts. Markings of cursus rhythms, and in the Apology of clausular rhythms, are mine. As in the preceding outline of the structure the parts in boldface roman numerals **I-V** and the chapter numbers in plain roman numerals I-XXVI are mine and putatively Patrick's. The upper case letters A-N-A' show which chapters are paired. To the left of the text in the first column arabic numbers enclosed in round brackets (1-62) represent the traditional chapter numbers. The arabic numbers without brackets are my line numbers. Words *italicized* in the text and marked by lower case letters and lower case roman numerals ai-ii-bi-ii-b'i-ii-a'i-ii in the third column show parallel and chiastic connections within chapters. Words underlined in the text and marked by upper case letters A1-2-3-B-C in the second column show connections between chapters within discrete parts of the *Confessio* and between paired parts of the *Confessio* (note: the dotted line is broken at points where it would otherwise collide with descenders). Words in SMALL CAPITALS in the text but not marked to the left will be discussed in the analysis of chapters within discrete parts of the *Confessio*. Words in SANS SERIF in the text but not marked to the left will be discussed in the analysis of connected larger parts of the *Confessio*.

PART I

(1)   I   A

     1   2a   i   *EGO* . <u>**PATRICIUS**</u> . <u>**PECCATOR**</u> .
                     RÚSTICÍSSIMUS
                     ET minimus ómnium **fi**délium .
                     ET contemptibilissimus **á**pud **p**lúrimos .

             ii   *Patrem* habui . **C**alpórnium DIÁCONUM .
    5   iii   *FIlium* quendam **P**otíti . PRESBÝTERI .
                     qui fuit uico **B**ánnauen**t**a Bérniae .
                     Uillulam enim **p**rópe hábuit .
                     ubi égo CAPTÙRAM DÉDI .

         b   i   ANNORUM ERAM TUNC . FÉRE SÉDECIM .
10   ii iii   DEUM enim uérum *ignorábam* .
    3   iv   *et* <u>HIBERIONE</u> . IN CAPTIUITÁTE **a**ddúctus sum .
                     Cum TOT MILIA HOMINUM . **se**cundum mérita nóstra .
                         quia 'a DEO recessimus' .
             v   et 'praecepta eius non *custodiuimus*'.
15   c   **ET sa***cerdotibus nostris non oboediéntes fúimus* .
                     *qui nostram sa**lú**tem **a**dmonébant* .
         d   i   **ET** DOMINUS '*induxit* **super** *nos iram animationis suae* .
             ii   *et dispersit nos in* **gentibus**' *multis* . *etiam* 'USQUE AD
                         ULTIMUM TERRAE'.
            ii'   *Ubi nunc* **p***aruitas mea esse uidetur* INTER ÁLIENÍGENAS .
(2)   i'   **ET** *ibi* 'DOMINUS **a***peruit sensum*
                       INCREDULITATIS *meae*'.
         c'   ut uel sero *rememorárem delìcta méa* .
         b'   ii   **ET** ut 'conuerterem toto corde ad DOMINUM DEUM
                     meum'.
             iv   qui 'respexit HUMILITATEM *meam*'.
    4   i iii   et *misertus est* ADOLESCENTIAE et *ignorántiae méae* .
25   v   **ET c***ustodiuit* me ÁNTEQUAM SCÌREM ÉUM .
                     ET ANTEQUAM SAPEREM uel distinguerem inter
                       bónum et málum .
                     ÉT muníuit me
28   a'i ii iii   et **c**onsolatus est *me* . ut *páter filium* .
(3)   II   B

     1   <u>Unde autem tacére non</u> póssum .
                     'neque expedit quidem'
                     tanta béneficia .
                     et tántam grátiam
    5   quam mihi Dominus praestáre dignátus est .
         2   'in <u>terra captiuitatis meae</u>'.
                     Quia haec est retribútio nóstra .
                     ut post correptionem uel ágnitiònem Déi
         3   '<u>exaltare</u> . et <u>confiteri mirabilia eius</u> .

PART I

I, Patrick, a sinner, very rustic,

and the least of all the faithful,
and very contemptible in the estimation of most men,
had as father a certain man called Calpornius, a deacon,
son of Potitus, a presbyter,
who was in the town Bannaventa Berniae,
for he had a little villa nearby,
where I conceded capture.
In years I was then almost sixteen.
For I was ignorant of the true God,
and I was led to Ireland in captivity
with so many thousands of men according to our deserts,
    because we withdrew from God,
and we did not keep watch over His precepts,
and we were not obedient to our priests,
who kept admonishing our salvation,
and the Lord led down over us the wrath of His anger
and dispersed us among many gentiles even as far as the furthest part of
    land,
where now my insignificance is seen to be among members of a strange race.
And there the Lord opened the consciousness of my unbelief

so that, perhaps, late, I might remember my delicts,
and that I might turn with a whole heart to the Lord my God,

Who turned His gaze round on my lowliness
and took pity on my adolescence and ignorance
and kept watch over me before I knew Him
and before I was wise or distinguished between good and bad,

and He fortified me
and consoled me as a father [consoles] a son.

Whence moreover I cannot be silent,
nor assuredly is it expedient,
about such great benefits
and such great grace,
which the Lord has deigned to supply to me
in the land of my captivity,
because this is our reward [lit. 'what is handed back']
as after rebuke and acknowledgement of God
to exalt and confess His marvels

10   coram . omni natione
         quae est sub omni caelo'.

(4) III   C   **Q**uia **n**on est álius Déus .
         nec úmquam fuit . ánte .
         nec érit . **p**óst haec .
         praeter Deum Pátrem ingénitum .
5   síne princípio .
         a quo est . ómne princípium .
         ómnia tenéntem .
         út didícimus .
         et huius filium Ièsum Xpístum .
10   quem cum Pátre scílicet
         semper fuísse testámur
         ante oríginem saéculi .
         spiritaliter apud Patrem . inenarrabíliter génitum
         ante ómne princípium .
15   et **p**er ipsum facta sunt uisibilia . et ínuisibília .
         hóminem fãctum .
         morte deuicta . in caelis ad Pátrem recéptum .

         '**E**t dedit illi omnem potestatem super omne nomen .
         caelestium .
20   et terrestrium .
         et infernorum .
         et omnis lingua confiteatur . ei
         quia Dominus et Deus est Iesus Xpistus'.
         Quem credimus .
25   et expectamus aduentum ípsius . **m**òx futúrum .
         '**I**udex uiuorum atque mortuorum .
         qui reddet unicuique secundum facta sua'.
         Et 'effudit in nobis . abunde Spíritum Sánctum
         donum' . et 'pignus' ínmortalitátis .
30   qui facit credentes . ét oboediéntes .
         ut sint 'filii Dei' et 'coheredes Xpisti' .
         quem confitémur et àdorámus .
         unum Deum in Trinitate sácri nóminis .

(5) IIII   D
1   **I**pse enim díxit per prophétam .
2   '**I**nuoca me in die tribulationis tuae .
         et liberabo te .
         et magnificabis me' .
5   **E**t íterum ínquit .
         '**O**pera autem Dei . reuelare et confiteri .
         honorificum est'.

before every nation
which is under every heaven.
Because there is not another God,
nor ever was before
nor will be after these [times],
besides God the unbegotten Father
without beginning,
from Whom is all beginning,
holding all things,
as we have learned,
and His Son Jesus Christ,
Whom with the Father, to be sure,
we bear witness always to have existed
before the origin of the age,
spiritually begotten with the Father in a way that cannot be narrated,
before all beginning,
and through Him have all things been made, visible and invisible,
made man,
when death had been utterly conquered, received in the heavens with the
    Father.
And He has given to Him all power over every name
of beings celestial
and terrestrial
and of the lower regions,
and every tongue should confess to Him
that Jesus Christ is Lord and God,
Whom we believe,
and we look hopefully for His advent, soon to be,
the judge of the living and the dead,
Who will give back to each according to his own deeds,
and He has poured out abundantly among us the Holy Spirit,
a gift and pledge of immortality,
Who makes those believing and obeying
that they may be sons of God and fellow heirs of Christ,
Whom we confess and adore,
one God in a Trinity of sacred name.

For He Himself has said through the prophet,
Call on me in the day of your tribulation
and I will free you
and you will magnify me.
And again He affirms,
To reveal and confess, moreover, the works of God
is a thing that confers honour.

(6) V   E
    1

Tamen etsi in multis ímperféctus sum .

opto 'fratribus et cognatis' meis scire quálitátem
    méam .

ut possint perspicere uotum ánimae méae .

(7) VI   F
    1

Non ignoro 'testimonium Domini mei' .

qui in psálmo testátur .

'Perdes eos qui loquuntur mendacium'.

Et íterum . ínquit

5   2

'Os quod mentitur . occidit animam' .

Et idem Dominus in euangélio ínquit .

'Uerbum otiosum quod locuti fuerint . homines .

reddent pro eo rationem in die iudicii'.

(8)

Unde autem ueheménter debúeram .

10

'cum timore et tremore' metuere . hánc senténtiam

in die illa . ubi nemo se poterit subtrahere . uél abscóndere .

Sed omnes omnino 'reddituri sumus rationem'.

etiam minimórum peccatórum .

'Ante tribunal Domini Xpisti'.

(9) VII

    a

Quapropter olim *cogitáui* scríbere .

sed et 'usque nûnc' haesitáui .

    b

Timui enim ne *'inciderem in LÍNGUAM'* hóminum .

quia *non didici* 'sícut' et 'céteri'.

5

qui optime itaque *iura* et sácras lítteras

utraque pari módo *combibérunt* .

    c

ET *SERMONES* illorum ex infantia númquam mutárunt .

sed magis 'ad perfectum' sémper addidérunt .

    d

Nam 'SERMO et loquela' nostra . *translata est ÍN*
    LÍNGUAM LIÉNAM .

10

Sicut facile potest probari ex salíua scriptúrae méae .

qualiter 'sum ego' in SERMONIBUS instructus átque
    'erudítus'.

quia inquit 'Sapiens Per LÍNGUAM dinoscétur .

et sensus . et scientia . et doctrína ueritátis'.

(10)   e

Sed quid prodest excusatio 'iúxta ueritátem'.

15

praesertim cûm praesúmptióne .

quatenus modo ipse adpeto 'in sénectúte' méa .

quod *'in iuuentute'* nón *comparáui* .

quod obstiterunt peccata méa . ut cónfirmárem

quod ánte perlégeram .

20

Sed quis me credit ? etsi dixero quod ánte praefátus sum ?

    2   a

ADOLESCENS . immo *paene púer* . *ínuerbis*

Nevertheless even if I am imperfect in many respects,
I prefer for my brothers and relatives to know my quality,

that they may see through to the vow of my soul.

I am not ignorant of the testimony of my Lord,
Who in the psalm testifies,
You will lose those who speak a lie.
And again He affirms,
The mouth which lies murders the soul.
And the same Lord in the Gospel affirms
The idle word which men will have spoken,
they will give back for it an account on the day of judgement.
Whence, moreover, I ought vehemently
with fear and trembling to fear this sentence
on that day where no man will have been able to withdraw or hide himself,
but we are all entirely bound to give back an account,
even of the least sins,
before the tribunal of the Lord Christ.

On which account formerly I thought about writing,
but even until now I hesitated,
for I feared lest I should fall onto the tongue of men,
because I did not learn just as the others also,
who most excellently, consequently, drank in laws and sacred letters,
both in equal measure,
and never changed their styles of speech from infancy,
but rather added always toward perfection.
For our speech and spoken language was translated into a strange tongue,

as it can easily be proved from the savour of my writing
how I was instructed and brought out from an uncultivated state in styles
    of speech,
because it affirms Through the tongue will the wise man be recognised,
also consciousness and knowledge and teaching of the truth.
But with respect to the truth what does an excuse profit,
particularly with obstinacy,
since now in my old age I seek
what in my youth I did not establish,
because my sins stood in the way that I should confirm
what I had read through before?
But who believes me even if I shall have said what I mentioned before?
As an adolescent, more precisely, as an almost wordless boy,

	b		CAPTÚRAM DÉDI .
	c		ANTEQUAM SCIREM QUÍD ADPÉTERE .
			uel quid uitáre debúeram .
25	d		Unde ergo hódie èrubésco .
			et ueheménter pertímeo
			denudare . imperítiam méam .
			quia disertis breuitate 'sermone explicáre' néqueo .
			Sicut enim spiritus géstit . et ánimus .
30			et sensus . mónstrat adféctus .
(11)	e		Sed si itaque datum mihi fuisset 'sícut' et 'céteris'.
			uerumtamen non silerem 'propter retributionem' .

3			Et si forte uidetur apud aliquantos me in hóc praepónere .
			Cum mea inscientia et 'tardiori LINGUA'.
35			sed etiam scríptum ést enim .
			'LINGUAE . balbutientes . uelociter discent loqui pacem'.
			quanto magis nos adpetere debémus . qui sùmus ínquit
			'Epistola[16] XPISTI in salutem . USQUE AD
			ULTIMUM TERRAE' .
			Et si non diserta . sed ráta . et fortíssima
40			'scripta in cordibus uestris .
			non atramento . sed SPIRITU DEI uiui'.
			Et iterum SPÍRITUS TESTÁTUR .
			'ET RUSTICATIONEM ab ALTISSIMO Creatam'.
(12) 2'	a		Unde ego prímus RÚSTICUS .
45	b		profuga . indóctus scílicet .
	c		'qui nescio in posterum prouidere' .
			Sed illud 'scio certissime . quia' utique 'priusquam
			HUMILIARER' .
			ego eram uelut lapis qui iacet in 'luto profundo'.
	d		et uénit 'qui pótens est'.
50			et in 'sua misericórdia' sustúlit me .
			ET quidem scilicet súrsum adleuáuit .
			et collocauit me in súmmo paríete .
	e		Et inde fortiter debúeram èxclamáre .
			'ad retribuendum' quoque áliquid 'DÓMINO'.
55			pro tantis beneficiis eius . híc et in aetérnum .
			quae mens hominum aestimáre nón potest .
(13) 1'a	i		Unde autem admirámini . ítaque
	ii iii iv		'magni et PUSILLI . qui timetis DEUM' .
	iii' ii'		et uos domini cáti rethórici .
60		i'	Audite ergo ét scrutámini .
	b		quis me stultum excitauit de médio eórum .
			qui uidentur esse sapientes et légis períti .

---

16 The Book of Armagh reads *Aepistola*.

I conceded capture
before I knew what I ought to seek
or what to avoid.
Whence therefore today I blush for shame
and vehemently thoroughly fear
to strip naked my unlearnedness,
because I cannot unfold in speech to those learned in conciseness
as, however, my spirit and mind longs,
and the emotion of my consciousness suggests.
But if, consequently, it had been given to me just as also to others,
even so I would not be silent on account of what should be handed back
    [from me to God].
And if by chance it seems to certain men that I put myself forward in this,
with my lack of knowledge and my rather slow tongue,
but even so it is, however, written
Stammering tongues will swiftly learn to speak peace.
How much more ought we to seek, we who are, he affirms,
The letter of Christ for salvation as far as the furthest part of land,

and if not learned, yet valid and very vigorous,
written in your hearts
not with ink but by the Spirit of the living God,
and again the Spirit testifies
even rustic work created by the Most High.
Whence I, the extreme rustic,
a refugee, untaught, doubtless,
who do not know how to look forward into the future,
but that I do know most certainly, that indeed before I was humbled

I was like a stone that lies in deep mud,
and He Who is powerful came
and in His pity He raised me up
and assuredly to be sure lifted me upward
and placed me on the highest wall
and therefore I ought forcefully to shout out
for something that should be handed back to the Lord also
for His benefits so great here and for eternity,
which [benefits] the mind of men cannot estimate.
Whence, moreover, be astonished, consequently,
you great and small who fear God,
and you, sirs [lords], clever rhetoricians,
hear therefore and examine
who roused me up, a fool, from the midst of those
who seem to be wise and learned by experience in law

        c   et '**p**otentes *in sermóne*' et **i**n ómni re .

    d *ia*   *Et* me quidem detestabilis huius mundi prae céteris
                       ìnspiráuit

65   *Si talis essem* . **D**úmmodo aútem

        b   *ut* '**c**um metu et reuerentia'.

                    et '**s**ine querella' **fi**deliter prodéssem *génti* .

                    ad quam '**c**aritas XPÍSTI' *transtúlit* .

        c   et *donauit me* in uita mea *si* dígnus fúero .

70   ii   **D**enique *ut* CUM HUMILITATE . et ueraciter *déseruírem íllis* .

(14)   iii*a*   **I**n '**m**ensura'. **i**taque 'fidei' TRINITATIS óportet
                     distínguere .

                    sine reprehensióne perículi .

        b   *notum fácere* '*dònum* DÉI .

      iv   et '**C**onsolationem **a**eternam' .

75   iii'*a*   *Síne timóre* .

        b   **FI**ducialiter *DEI* nomen úbique *expándere* .

      ii'   *Ut* etiam 'POST OBITUM MEUM' *exagallias relinquere fratribus*
                    et filiis méis .

                    quos in DOMINO **e**go baptizaui TOT MÍLIA
                    HÓMINUM .

(15) i'*a*   *Et non eram* dígnus neque *tális* .

80   b   *ut* hoc DOMINUS seruulo súo concéderet .

                    post aerúmnas . et **t**àntas móles .

                    PÓST CAP**T**IUITÁTEM .

                    Post annos múltos *in* gèntem íllam

        c   tantam **g**ratiam *míhi donáret* .

85   a   **Q**uod ego aliquando *in iuuentute* mea *numquam speraui*
                    néque *cogitáui* .

PART II

(16) VIII G   1

    1   **S**ed postquam HIBERIÓNE deuéneram .

    2   cotidie . **i**taque pécora pascébam .

                    et frequens in díe ORÁBAM .

        a b   **M**agis ac magis accedebat amor *Dei* . et *tímor* ípsius .

5   c   et *fides* augebatur . et SPÍRITUS . àgebátur .

                    ut in die una usque ad céntum ORÀTIÓNES .

                    et in nocte própe simíliter .

                    ut etiam in siluis et mónte manébam .

                    et ante lucem excitabar ád ORÁTIÓNEM .

10   per niuem . per gélu . per plúuiam .

                    et nihil máli sentiébam .

                    neque ulla pigrítia èrat ín me .

and powerful in speech and in everything
and inspired me, assuredly, beyond the others of this execrable world

if I should be such — if only moreover [I were] —
that with fear and reverence
and without complaint I should proceed faithfully to that gentile people
to which the charity of Christ translated me
and granted me during my life, if I will have been worthy,
that at last with humility and truthfully I might serve them.
According to the measure, consequently, of the faith of the Trinity it is
   fitting to distinguish,
without blame of danger [by hypallage 'without danger of blame', *i.e.*
   'without fear of criticism']
to make known the gift of God
and [His] eternal consolation,
without fear
in faithworthy fashion to expound everywhere the name of God,
in order even after my death to leave behind a legacy to my brothers and
   sons
whom I have baptized in the Lord, so many thousands of men.

And I was not worthy nor such
that the Lord should allow this to His little servant,
after troubles and such great burdens,
after captivity,
after many years among that gentile people,
that He should grant such great grace to me,
which I never at any time in my youth hoped for nor thought about.

PART II

But after I had come to Ireland,
I was consequently pasturing domestic animals daily,
and often in the day I was praying.
More and more the love of God and fear of Him was approaching,
and faith was being increased, and the Spirit was being stirred up,
so that in a single day up to a hundred prayers,
and in a night nearly the same,
even as I was staying in forests and on the mountain,
and before dawn I was roused up to prayer,
through snow, through frost, through rain,
and I was feeling nothing bad,
nor was there any sloth in me,

sicut modo uideo . quia tunc SPIRITUS ín me feruébat .

(17) 3 et ibi scilicet quadam nócte in sómno

15 d i *Audiui* uócem dicèntem míhi .

ii "**B**ene ieiunas . cito *iturus* ad pátriam túam" .

iii *Et iterum post paúlulum témpus .*

iv *audiui 'respónsum' dicèntem míhi .*

e "*Ecce nauis túa paráta est*".

20 f *Et nón erat própe :*

sed forte habebat . ducenta mília pássus .

et ibi númquam fúeram .

nec ibi notum quemquam de homínibus habébam .

g *Et deinde postmodum conuérsus sum in fúgam .*

25 h *et intermisi hominem cum quo fúeram sex ánnis .*

h' *et ueni ín uirtúte Déi .*

g' *qui uiam meam ad bónum dirigébat .*

f'e' *et nihil metuebam donec peruéni ad nàuem íllam .*

(18) **E**t illa die qua perueni profecta est náuis de lòco súo .

30 et locutus sum ut haberem *unde nauigáre cum íllis .*

et **g**ubernator . displícuit . ílli .

Et acriter cum indignatióne respóndit .

d' ii "**N**equaquam tu nobiscum ádpetes *íre*".

i **E**t cum haec *audiissem* . separáui me ab íllis .

35 ut uenirem **a**d teguriolum . úbi hospitábam .

et in itinere coépi ORÁRE .

4 iii *Et antequam ORATIÓNEM consummárem .*

iv *Audiui únum ex íllis*

et fortiter éxclamábat póst me .

40 "**U**eni cito . quia uocant te hómines ísti".

Et statim ad íllos reuérsus sum .

et coeperunt míhi dícere .

c' "**U**eni quia ex *fide* recipimus te [? l. té recípimus] .

fac nobiscum amicitiam quo módo uolúeris".

45 **E**t in illa die itaque reppuli 'sugere mammellas . eorum'

b'a' própter *timòrem Déi .*

Sed uerumtamen ab illis speraui . uenire in fidem Iésu

Xpísti .

Quía géntes érant .

et ob hoc obtínui cum íllis .

50 et protinus *náuigáuimus .*

(19) 2

Et post triduum térram cépimus .

1 et uiginti octo dies per desertum íter fécimus .

as I see now, because the Spirit was being fervent in me then,
and there, to be sure, on a certain night in a dream
I heard a voice saying to me,
"It is well that you are fasting, bound soon to go to your fatherland".
And again after a very little time
I heard the answer saying to me,
"Look, your ship is ready".
And it was not near,
but perhaps two hundred miles [lit. 'it had two hundred thousand double
    paces'],
and I had never been there,
nor did I have any single acquaintance among men there,
and then later I turned to flight,
and I abandoned the man with whom I had been for six years,
and I came in the power of God,
Who was directing my way toward the good,
and I was fearing nothing until I came through to that ship,
and on that day on which I came through the ship set out from its own
    place,
and I spoke as I had the wherewithal to ship with them,
and the captain, it displeased him,
and he responded sharply with indignation,
"By no means will you seek to go with us".
And when I heard these things I separated myself from them,
so that I would come to the little hut where I was staying,
and on the journey I began to pray,
and before I could bring the prayer to the highest perfection
I heard one of them,
and he was shouting out vigorously after me,
"Come soon, because these men are calling you",
and immediately I returned to them,
and they began to say to me,
"Come, because we are receiving you on faith,
make friendship with us in whatever way you will have wished",
and on that day, to be sure, I refused to suck their nipples
on account of the fear of God,
but nevertheless I hoped to come by them to the faith of Jesus Christ,

as they were gentiles,
and because of this I got my way with them,
and we shipped at once.

And after a three-day period we reached land,
and for twenty-eight days we made a journey through the desert,

3	a	i	*et cibus défuit íllis* .
		ii	*et 'fames inualuit super eos'* .

55   Et alio die coepit gubernator míhi dícere .

"**Q**uíd est Xpístiáne **?**

bi ii iii iv   *Tu dicis Deus tuus magnus et ómnipótens est* **?**

Quare ergo non potes pro nóbis ORÁRE **?**

c   *Quia nos a fame périclitámur* **?**

60   2   **D**ifficile est enim . ut aliquem hominem úmquam uideámus".

b' i ii   **E**go enim confidénter *dixi* íllis .

iii   "'**C**onuertemini' ex fide . 'ex toto corde a**d** Dóminum *Dèum méum* .

iv   *quia nihil est impossíbile . illi'.*

3   a   i   *ut hodie cibum mittat uobis* in UIAM uestram usque dúm satiámini .

65   ii   *quia ubique ábundábat ílli*".

3

1   a   **E**t[17] *ADIUUANTE DEO* . íta fáctum est .

b   i   **E**cce *grex porcorum in UIA ANTE OCULOS* nóstros appáruit .[18]

ii   *et multos ex illis ínterfecérunt .*

2   c   *Et ibi duas noctes manserunt . et béne refécti .*

70   et carne eórum repléti sunt .

quia multi ex íllis 'defecérunt'.

et secus UIAM 'semiuíui relícti' sunt .

d   *Et post hoc SUMMAS GRATIAS EGÉRUNT DÉO .*

d'   *et ego honorificatus sum SUB ÓCULIS EÓRUM .*

75   3   c'   *et e**x** hac die . cibum abundánter habuérunt .*

b'   i   **E**tiam *'mel siluéstre' inuenérunt .*

ii   *et 'mihi partem obtulerunt' .*

Et unus ex illis dixit . "'Ímmolatícium est'".

a'   *DÉO GRÁTIAS .*

80   exinde níhil gustáui .

(20) 4

a   **E**adem *uero nocte* éram dórmiens .

b   *ET fortiter TEMPTÁUIT ME SÁTANAS .*

quod memor ero 'quamdiu fuero in hoc corpore'.

c   *Et cecidit super me uéluti sàxum íngens .*

85   et nihil membrorum meórum praéualens .

d   i   **S**ed unde me uenit . ignaro . in spiritu *ut Héliam uocárem .*

ii   **E**t inter haec *uidi in caelum sólem oríri .*

d'   i   et *dum clamarem "Helia, Helia"* uíribus méis .

ii   **E**cce *splendor solis illius decídit súper me .*

90   c'   *et statim discussit a me omnem gráuitúdinem .*

b'   *et credo quod a Xpisto Domino méo subuéntus sum .*

---

17   MS C omits *Et* and reads *Adiuuante*.   18   MS C omits *apparuit* and reads *nostros*.

and food was not forthcoming for them,
and hunger prevailed over them,
and on the next day the captain began to say to me,
"What is it, Christian?
You say your God is great and all-powerful.
Why therefore can you not pray for us,
because we are imperilled by hunger,
for it is not likely that we may ever see any man".

But I said confidently to them,
"Be turned in faith with a whole heart to the Lord my God,

because nothing is impossible to Him,
so that today He may dispatch food to you until you should be satisfied on
    your way,
as there was abundance everywhere for Him".

And with God helping it was made so.
Look, a flock of pigs appeared in the way before our eyes,
and they killed many of them,
and there they remained two nights and were well fed,
and they were refilled with their flesh,
because many of them fainted away,
and were left behind half-alive along the way,
and after this they gave the highest thanks to God,
and I was made honourable in their eyes,
and from this day they had food abundantly;
they even discovered [lit. 'came upon'] forest honey,
and they offered a part to me,
and one of them said, "It is a [pagan] sacrifice".
Thanks be to God,
I tasted nothing from it.

But on the same night I was sleeping,
and Satan tried me vigorously,
which I shall be mindful of as long as I will have been in this body,
and he fell over me like a huge rock,
and none of my members having any prevailing power.
But whence came to me in my ignorant spirit that I should call Elias?
And amidst these things I saw the sun rise into the heaven,
and while I was calling "Elia, Elia" with all my powers,
look, the splendour of His sun [ἥλιος] fell down over me,
and immediately shook off from me all oppressiveness,
and I believe that I was come to the aid of by Christ my Lord,

            et SPIRITUS eius iam túnc clamábat pró me .

            Et spero quod sic erit 'in díe pressùrae' méae .

    a'   sicut in euangelio ínquit . *'In illa díe'*

95   Dominus TESTATUR . '**N**on uos estis qui loquimini .

            sed SPIRITUS Patris uestri qui loquitur in uobis'.

(21) 3'

            Et iterum . **P**ost annos multos adhúc CAPTURAM DÉDI .

  2   a   *Ea nocte prima* itaque mánsi cum íllis .

            '**R**esponsum' autem 'diuinum' **a**udíui dicèntem míhi .

100 2 b "**D**uobus mensibus éris cum íllis".

  1 c *Quod íta fáctum est .*

      b' *Nocte illa séxagésima .*

            'liberauit me Dominus de manibus eorum' .

(22) 3   **Et**iam in itinere praeuídit nobis cíbum .

105   et ignem . et siccitátem cotídie .

    a'   donec *decimo die* peruénimus hómines .

  2'

  1   Sicut superius ínsinuáui .

            Uiginti et octo dies per desertum íter fécimus .

  2 3   et ea nocte qua peruenimus homines . *de cibo uero níhil*

             habúimus .

(23) 1'

110 1   **Et** iterum post paucos annos in Brittánniis éram

  2   cum paréntibus méis .

         qui me ut filium sùscepérunt .

     a i et ex fide *rogauérunt me*

        ii *ut* uel modo ego post tantas tribulationes quas égo pertúli .

115   iii *nusquam ab íllis discéderem .*

  3   **Et** ibi scilicet 'uidi in uisu noctis' uirum uenientem quasi

            dé Hiberióne

         cui nomen Uíctorícius

         cum epistolis innúmerabílibus .

         et dedit míhi . únam éx his

120 aiv bi ii *et legi . **P**rincipium epistolae continentem . 'Uox Hibérionácum'.*

   c b'i *Et cum recitabam princípium epístolae .*

       ii putabam . ipso momento audire *uócem ipsórum*

         qui erant iuxta síluam Uoclúti .

         quae est prope mare óccidentále .

125   et sic exclamauerunt 'quasi ex uno ore'.

    a' i "**R**ogámus te sàncte púer .

   ii iii *ut uenias et adhuc ámbulas . ínter nos" .*

         Et ualde 'compunctus sum corde'.

     iv *et amplius non pótui légere .*

130 a" i *Et síc expértus sum*

and His Spirit was already then shouting for me,
and I hope that it will be so on the day of my pressing need,
as He affirms in the Gospel, On that day,
the Lord testifies, You will not be you who speak
but the Spirit of your Father Who speaks in you.

And again after many years farther I conceded capture.
Consequently on that first night I remained with them
I heard moreover a divine answer saying to me,
"For two months you will be with them",
which was made so.
On that sixtieth night
the Lord freed me from their hands.
He even foresaw for us on the journey food
and fire and dryness daily,
until on the tenth day we came through to men.

As I have made known above,
we made a journey through the desert twenty and eight days,
and on that night on which we came through to men we had in truth
   nothing of food.

And again after a few years in the Britains I was
with my parents,
who received me as a son,
and in faith requested me
whether now I, after such great tribulations which I bore,
I should not ever depart from them.
And there to be sure I saw in a vision of the night a man coming as if from
   Ireland,
whose name [was] Victoricius,
with innumerable epistles,
and he gave me one of them,
and I read the beginning of the epistle containing 'the Voice of the Irish',
and while I was reciting the beginning of the epistle
I kept imagining hearing at that very moment the voice of those very men
who were beside the Forest of Foclut,
which is near the Western Sea [lit. 'the sea of the setting (*sc.* of the sun)'],
and thus they shouted out as if from one mouth,
"We request you, holy boy,
that you come and walk farther among us".
And I was especially stabbed at heart,
and I could not read further.
And thus I have learned by experience,

Déo grátias .

quia post plurimos annos praestitit íllis Dóminus
secundum clamórem illórum .

(24)   Et alia nocte 'nescio Deus scit'.

135   utrum ín me an iúxta me

       ii   *uerbis peritissimis quos égo audíui*
            et non potui íntellégere .

   4   b"   *nisi ad postremum ORATIONIS síc effitiátus est .*
       c"   *"'Qui dedit animam suam pro te'.*

140   *ipse est qui lóquitur ín te"*

          et sic expergefactus súm gaudibúndus .

(25)   d"   Et iterum uidi in me ípsum ORÁNTEM .

          et eram quasi íntra córpus méum .

          Et audiui super me hoc est super 'interiorem hominem'.

145   et ibi fortiter ORÁBAT gemítibus .

          Et inter haec 'stupebam et admirabam . et cogitabam'

       c'''   *quis esset quí in me ORÁBAT .*

   4   b'''   *Sed ad postremum ORATIONIS . sic effitiatus est* út sit
           SPÍRITUS .

     a'''i   *Et síc expértus sum*

150   et recordatus sum apóstolo dicénte .

          'SPIRITUS adiuuat infirmitates ORATIONIS nostrae .

          Nam quod OREMUS sicut oportet nescimus .

          sed ipse SPIRITUS postulat pro nobis gemitibus
           inenarrabilibus .

       ii   *quae uerbis exprimi non possunt'.*

155   Et iterum . 'Dominus aduocatus noster . postulat pro
          nobis'.

PART III

(26) VIIII H

   1   a   ET quando *TEMPTATUS SUM AB ALIQUANTIS*
          SENIORIBUS MÉIS qui uenérunt .

          et peccata mea contra laboriosum EPISCOPATUM
           méum obiecérunt .

       b   utique illo die fórtiter 'impúlsus sum
          ut caderem'. híc et in aetérnum .

5   2   sed Dominus pepercit proselíto et pèregríno

     3   propter nomen súum benígne .

          et ualde mihi subuenit in hac cónculcatióne .

     4   Quod in labe et in obprobrium non mále deuéni

       c   *Deum oro . ut 'non illis in peccatum reputetur'*

(27)   d   *'Occasionem'. Post annos triginta . 'inuenerunt me . aduersus'*

thanks be to God,
that after very many years the Lord has supplied them
according to their clamour.
And on another [or 'the second'] night, I do not know, God knows,
whether within me or beside me,
in most learned words I heard those whom
I could not yet understand,
except that at the very end of the prayer one spoke out thus:
"He Who has given His own soul for you
He it is Who speaks in you",
and thus I was awakened rejoicing.
And again I saw Him praying within myself,
and I was as if inside my body,
and I heard over me, this is, over the interior man,
and there He was praying vigorously with groans,
and amidst these things I was stupefied and I kept marvelling and thinking
Who He might be Who was praying in me,
but at the very end of the prayer thus He spoke out that He might be the
 Spirit.
And thus I have learned by experience
and recalled to mind, as the apostle says,
The Spirit helps the weaknesses of our prayer.
For we do not know, as is fitting, what we should pray for,
but the Spirit Himself demands for us with groans that cannot be narrated

things which cannot be expressed in words.
And again, The Lord our advocate demands for us.

PART III

And when I was tried by certain of my elders who came

and hurled my sins as a charge against my toilsome episcopate,

indeed on that day I was vigorously pushed back,
so that I should fall here and for eternity,
but the Lord spared a sojourner and exile
on account of His own kindly name,
and especially came to my support in this trampling down,
so that in collapse and in shame I did not come out badly.
I pray God that it not be reckoned to them as sin.
After thirty years they discovered [lit. 'came upon', 'invented'] an occasion

	e	*uerbum quod confessus fueram antequam éssem* . DIÁCONUS .
5	f	*Propter anxietatem maesto* **animo** *insinuaui* AMICÍSSIMO MÉO

	e'	*quae in pueritia mea una díe gésseram* .
		Ímmo in ùna hóra
15		quia nécdum praeualébam.
		'Nescio Deus scit'.
	d'	SI *HABEBAM TUNC ÁNNOS QUÍNDECIM* .
	c'	et *Deum* uíuum non credébam .
		neque ex infántia méa .
20	6	sed in morte et IN INCREDÚLITÁTE mánsi
	b'	donec ualde *cástigátus sum* .
	a'	'et in ueritate HUMÍLIÁTUS SUM
		a fame et nuditáte'. et cotídie

(28) X	J	
		Contra Hiberione non spónte pergébam .
	1	'donec' prope 'deficiebam' .
		Sed hoc potius béne mihi fúit .
		qui ex hoc emendátus sum a Dómino .
5	2	et aptauit me ut hódie éssem .
		quod aliquando lónge **a** mé erat .
	3	ut ego cúram habérem .
		aut satagerem pro salúte aliórum
		quando **a**utem tunc etiam de me ipso nón cogitábam .

(29) XI	K	
		Igitur in illo die quo 'reprobatus sum'.
		A memorátis supradíctis .
		ad noctem illam 'uidi in uisu noctis' .
		quod scriptum erat contra faciem meam síne honóre .
5	1	Et inter haec audiui 'responsum diuínum' dicèntem míhi .
		"Male uidimus faciem designati . nudáto nómine".

		nec sic praedixit "Mále uidísti".
		sed "Mále uídimus"
		quasi síbi me iunxísset .
10	2	sicut dixit . 'Qui uos tangit .
		Quasi qui tangit pupillam oculi mei'.

(30) XII	L	
	1	Idcirco 'gratias ago ei
	2	qui me' in ómnibus 'cònfortáuit' .
		ut non me impediret a profectione quám statúeram .

	3	Et de mea quoque opera quod a Xpisto Domino méo

against me,
a word which I had confessed before I was a deacon.
On account of anxiety in a mournful mind I made known to my most
    intimate friend
what I had done in my boyhood on one day,
more precisely in one hour,
because I had not yet prevailing power.
I do not know, God knows
if I then had fifteen years,
and I did not believe the living God,
nor [had I believed] from my infancy,
but I remained in death and in unbelief
until the time I was especially castigated,
and in truth I was humiliated
by hunger and nakedness, even daily.

On the other hand I did not proceed to Ireland with willing consent
until the time I nearly fainted away.
But this was rather well for me,
who have because of this been freed from a fault by the Lord,
and He has fitted me so that today I may be
what was once far away from me,
that I may have the care
or rather be occupied with the salvation of others,
when moreover at that time I was not thinking even about myself.

So then on that day on which I was reproved
by those called to mind, the abovesaid,
on that night I saw in a vision of the night
what had been written against my face without honour,
and amidst these things I heard the divine answer saying to me,
"We have seen badly [*i.e.*'with disapproval'] the face of the man marked
    out with his name stripped naked",
and He did not say forth, "You have seen badly",
but "We have seen badly",
as if He had joined me to Himself,
just as He has said, "He who touches you
[is] as he who touches the pupil of my eye".

Because of that I give thanks to Him
Who has strengthened me in all things,
so that He did not impede me from setting out on the journey which I had
    decided on,
and also from my task which I had learned from Christ my Lord,

didíceram .

5   sed magis ex eo 'sensi in me uirtútem' non páruam .

    4   et fides mea probata est coram Déo et homínibus .

(31) XIII M

    1   **U**nde autem 'audenter dico'.

         Non me reprehendit consciéntia méa .

         híc et in futúrum .

    2   3   'Teste Déo' hábeo

5   'quia non sum mentitus'

         in sermonibus quos égo retùli uóbis .

(32) XIIII N

     Sed magis doleo pro AMICÍSSIMO MÉO .

     cur hoc meruimus audire tále respónsum .

     Cui ego credidi étiam ánimam.

     Et comperi AB ALIQUÁNTIS FRÁTRIBUS .

5   **A**nte defénsiónem íllam

     quod ego nón intérfui .

     nec in Brittánniis éram .

        a   nec a *me* óriebátur .

       bc   ut et *ille in méa abséntia pulsáret pró me* .

10   d   etiam mihi . *Ipse ore súo díxerat* .

       d'   *"Ecce dandus es tu ad grádum EPÌSCOPÁTUS".*

       c'   *quod nón eram dígnus* .

       b'   **S**ed unde uenit *ílli* póstmodum

         ut coram cunctis bónis et mális

15   a'   et *me* publice déhonestáret .

         quod ante sponte et laétus indúlserat .

         Et Dominus qui 'maior omnibus est'.

(33) XV M'

    1   **S**atis 'dico' .

         Sed tamen non debeo abscóndere 'dònum Déi'

         quod largitus est nobis 'in terra captiuitatis meae'.

         quia tunc fortiter ínquisíui éum .

5   et íbi inuèni íllum .

         et seruauit me ab omnibus iníquitátibus .

         Sic credo 'propter inhabitantem Spíritum' eíus .

         qui 'operatus est' usque in hánc diem ín me [? l. in me

             úsque in hanc díem] .

    1   'Audénter' rúrsus .

10   2   **S**ed scit Deus si mihi homo hoc effátus fuísset .

    3   forsitan tacuissem propter 'caritatem Xpisti' .

(34) XVI L'

    1   a   *Unde ergo indefessam gratiam ágo Déo méo* .

  2 4   b   *qui me fidelem seruauit 'in die temptátiónis' méae* .

but rather from Him I sensed within myself a not insignificant power,
and my faith was approved before God and men.

Whence moreover I say boldly
my conscience does not reprehend me
here and for the future.
I have with God as witness
that I have not lied
in the speeches which I have referred to you.

But I grieve the more for my most intimate friend,
because we deserved to hear such an answer from this man,
to whom I entrusted even my soul.
And I have discovered from certain brothers
before that defence,
because I was not present,
nor was I in the Britains,
nor did it arise from me,
that he also in my absence would importune for me.
He himself had even said to me from his own mouth,
"Look, you are to be given over to the grade of the episcopate",
which I was not worthy of.
But whence did it come to him afterwards
that in the sight of all, good and bad,
he should dishonour me even publicly
over something he had conceded before happy and with willing consent,
and the Lord, Who is greater than all.

I say enough.
But nevertheless I ought not to hide the gift of God,
which has been granted to us in the land of my captivity,
because then I vigorously sought Him,
and there I found Him,
and He kept me from all iniquities, so I believe,
on account of His indwelling Spirit,
Who has worked up to this day in me.

Boldly again.
But, God knows, if a man had spoken this out to me,
perhaps I would have been silent about the charity of Christ.

Whence therefore I give unwearied thanks to my God,
Who has kept me faithful on the day of my trial,

3	c		*ita ut hodie confidenter offeram illi sácrifícium* .
3	c'		*ut 'hostiam uiuentem' animam meam . Xpisto Dómino méo* .
5 2	b'		*qui me 'seruauit ab omnibus angustiis meis'* .

Ut et dicam . 'Quis ego sum Domine'.

uel quae est uocátio méa .

qui mihi tanta diuinitáte compàruísti .

ita ut hódie 'in géntibus'.

10   constánter 'exaltárem .

et magnificárem . nómen túum'

ubicumque lóco fúero .

Nec nón in secúndis .

sed étiam in pressúris .

15   Ut quicquid míhi euénerit .

siue bónum siue málum .

1   a'   *Aequaliter débeo suscípere* .

            et Deo gratias sémper ágere .

2   b"   *qui míhi osténdit*

20   ut indubitabilem eum sine fine créderem .

Et qui mé audíerit

ut ego inscius et 'in nouissimis diebus'.

3   c"   *Hoc opus tam pium et tam mirificum* audérem adgrédere .

ita ut imitarem quíppiam íllos .

25   quos ante Dominus iam ólim praedíxerat

praenuntiaturos . euangélium súum

'in testimonium omnibus gentibus' ánte 'finem múndi'.

quod ita ergo uidimus . ítaque supplétum est .

Ecce testes sumus . quia euangelium praédicátum est .

30   usque ubi némo última est .

(35) XVII K'

Longum est autem totum per singula enarrare laborem
      méum . uel per pártes

Breuiter dicam qualiter piissimus Deus de seruitute saépe
      liberáuit .

Et de periculis duodecim qua periclitata est ánima méa .

praeter insídias múltas .

5   Et 'quae uerbis exprimere non ualeo'

Nec iniuriam legéntibus fáciam .

sed Deum auctórem hábeo

qui nouit omnia etiam ántequam fiant .

2   ut me paupérculum pupíllum .

10   1   Idiotam 'responsum diuinum' crébre admonére .

(36) XVIII J'

2   'Unde mihi haec sapientia'

quaé in me nón erat

so that today I may confidently offer sacrifice to Him,
my soul as a living host to Christ my Lord,
Who has kept me from all my straits,
so that I also may say, "Who am I, Lord,
or what is my calling",
[You] Who have appeared to me with such divinity,
so that today among gentiles
I may constantly exalt
and magnify Your name
in whatever place I shall have been
and not only in favourable circumstances,
but also in pressing needs,
so that whatever will have happened to me,
either good or bad,
I ought to undertake equally,
and always to give thanks to God,
Who has shown to me
that I should believe Him indubitable without end,
and He Who will have heard me,
so that I unknowing and in the final days
may dare to approach this work so pious and so wondrous,
so that I to some degree may imitate those
whom the Lord long before now had said beforehand
as going to herald His own Gospel,
as a testimonial to all the gentiles before the end of the world,
which we therefore have seen so, and so it has been fulfilled.
Look, we are testifiers that the Gospel has been proclaimed
as far as where there is no man beyond.

It is, moreover, longwinded to relate my labour by single examples, or in
    parts.
Briefly I shall say how the most pious God has often freed from slavery

and from twelve perils in which my soul was imperilled,
besides many treacheries
and things which I am not able to express in words.
I shall not make an injustice for those reading,
but I have God as authority,
Who knows all things even before they may be done,
that me, a poor little pupil,
an ordinary person [His] divine answer would frequently admonish.

Whence [came] to me this wisdom,
which was not in me,

1			qui nec 'numerum dierum noueram' .		

          neque Déum sapiébam .

5 3   Unde mihi postmodum donum tam mágnum tam salúbre

          Deum **a**gnoscere uél dilígere .

          Sed ut patriam et paréntes **a**mítterem .

(37) XVIIII H'

          Et munera multa mihi offerebantur cum flétu et lácrimis ét offéndi íllos .

1   nec non contra uotum ALIQUANTOS DE SENIÓRIBUS MÉIS .

          Sed gubernante Deo nullo modo consensi neque ádquieui íllis .

5   non mea gratia sed Déus qui uìncit ín me .

          et resistit íllis ómnibus .

          Ut ego ueneram ad Hibernas gentes euangélium praèdicáre .

6   et AB INCREDULIS contumélias perférre .

4 2   ut 'audirem obprobrium peregrinationis meae'.

10   et persecutiones multas 'usque ad uincula'.

          et ut darem ingenuitatem meam pro utilitáte aliórum .

          Et si dignus fúero . 'prómptus' sum .

5   ut etiam 'animam meam'

3   incunctanter et 'libentissime' pro nómine eíus .

PART IIII

(37) XX G'

1   Et ibi opto 'impendere' eam 'usque ad mortem' .

2   si Dominus míhi indulgéret .

(38) 3   quia ualde 'débitor sum' Déo

          qui mihi tantam grátiam donáuit .

5 4 1 ab   ut *populi* multi per me in Déum *renàsceréntur* .

          et postmodum cónsummaréntur .

2 c   **E**t ut *clerici* ubique illis órdinaréntur .

     d i   ad plebem nuper *uenientem* ád credúlitátem .

        ii quam sumpsit *Dominus* 'ab extremis terrae' .

10   iii **S**icut olim *promiserat pér prophétas* súos

        iv '*Ad te gentes . uenient ab extremis terrae et dicent* .

          "**S**icut falsa comparauerunt patres nostri idola .

          et non est in eis utilitas'".

          Et iterum . '**P**osui te lumen in gentibus .

15 3   ut sis in salutem usque **a**d extremum terrae'.

(39)   e   *Et ibi uolo 'expectare promíssum' ípsius*

          qui útique nùmquam fállit .

          sicut in euangélio pòllicétur .

who knew neither the number of days,
nor did I have any wisdom about God?
Whence [came] to me afterward the gift so great, so salutary,
to acknowledge or to love God dearly,
but that I would lose fatherland and parents?

And many gifts kept being offered to me with weeping and tears,
and I offended those [who gave them],
and also against [my] wish a certain number of my elders,

but with God acting as captain in no way did I agree with them nor
    acquiesce,
not by my grace but God Who conquers in me,
and stood firm against them all,
as I had come to Irish gentiles to proclaim the Gospel,
and to endure indignities from unbelievers,
so that I might hear shame of my exile,
and many persecutions up to the point of chains,
and so that I might give up my freeborn status for the advantage of others,
and if I will have been worthy I am quick to respond,
so that [I might give up] even my soul,
unhesitatingly and most willingly for His name.

PART IIII

And there I prefer to spend it up to the point of death,
if the Lord should concede to me,
because I am especially a debtor [lit. 'ower'] to God,
Who has granted to me such great grace,
that many people through me should be reborn to God,
and afterwards brought to the highest perfection,
and that clerics everywhere should be ordained for them,
for a folk coming recently to belief,
whom the Lord has taken up from the most remote parts of land,
just as formerly He had promised through His own prophets:
To you gentiles will come from the most remote parts of land, and they
    will say,
Our fathers established idols as false things,
and there is no advantage in them.
And again: I have placed you as a light among the gentiles,
so that you may be for salvation as far as the most remote part of land,
and there I wish to wait hopefully for the promise of Him,
Who indeed never deceives.
Just as He guaranteed in the Gospel,

'Uenient ab oriente et occidente .

20 et recumbent cum Abraham et Isaac et Iacob'.

d' i sicut credimus ab omni mundo *uentúri sunt credéntes* .

(40) Idcirco itaque oportet quidem bene et diligénter piscáre .

ii sicut *Dominus* praemónet et dòcet dícens .

'Uenite post me . et faciam uos fieri piscatores hominum' .

25 iii Et iterum *dícit per prophétas* .

iv *'Ecce mitto piscatores et uenatores multos dicit Déus'*. et cétera .

Unde autem ualde oportebat retia nóstra téndere .

ita ut 'multitudo copiosa et turba' Déo caperétur .

2 1 c'b' Et ubique essent *clerici qui báptizárent* .

30 a' et exhortarent *populum* indigentem ét desíderántem .

sicut Dominus inquit in éuangélio

admónet et dòcet dícens .

'Euntes ergo nunc docete omnes gentes .

baptizantes eas in nomine Patris et Filii et Spiritus Sancti .

35 Docentes eos obseruare omnia quaecumque mandaui uobis .

Et ecce ego uobiscum sum omnibus diebus .

usque ad consummationem saeculi'.

Et iterum dicit . 'Euntes ergo in mundum uniuersum .

praedicate euangelium omni creaturae .

40 Qui crediderit et baptizatus fuerit . saluus erit .

Qui uero non crediderit . condempnabitur'.

Et iterum . 'Praedicabitur hoc euangelium regni in

uniuerso mundo .

in testimonium omnibus gentibus .

et tunc ueniet finis'.

45 Et item Dominus per prophetam praenúntiat ínquit .

'Et erit in nouissimis diebus dicit Dominus .

Effundam de Spiritu meo super omnem carnem

et prophetabunt filii uestri et filiae uestrae .

et iuuenes uestri uisiones uidebunt .

50 et seniores uestri somnia somniabunt .

Et quidem super seruos meos .

et super ancillas meas . in diebus illis

effundam de Spiritu meo et prophetabunt'.

Et 'in Osee dicit . Uocabo non plebem meam plebem

meam .

55 et non misericordiam consecutam . misericordiam

consecutam .

Et erit in loco ubi dictum est . Non plebs mea uos .

ibi uocabuntur filii Dei uiui'.

(41) 5 Unde autem Hiberione . qui numquam notitiam Déi

habuérunt .

They will come from the rising and the setting [*i.e.* from east and west],
and they will lie back with Abraham and Isaac and Jacob,
just as we believe that those believing are bound to come from all the world.
Because of that consequently it is fitting assuredly to fish well and with
    loving care,
just as the Lord admonishes in advance and teaches, saying,
Come after me and I will make you to be made fishers of men,
and again He says through the prophets,
Look, I send fishers and many hunters, says God, and the other parts.
Whence moreover it was especially fitting to extend our nets,
so that a plentiful multitude and throng should be captured for God,
and everywhere there should be clerics who would baptize,
and exhort a needing and desiring people,
just as the Lord affirms in the Gospel,
He admonishes and teaches, saying,
Going therefore teach now all the gentiles,
baptizing them in the name of the Father and the Son and the Holy Spirit,
teaching them to observe all things whatsoever I have commanded to you,
and look, I am with you all days,
as far as the highest perfection of the age.
And again He says, Going therefore into the entire world,
proclaim the Gospel to every creature.
He who will have believed and been baptized will be saved,
but he who who will not have believed will be condemned.
And again, Proclaim this Gospel of the Realm in the entire world,

for testimony to all gentiles,
and then the end will come.
And similarly the Lord announces beforehand through the prophet, He affirms,
And it will be in the final days, says the Lord,
I will pour out from my Spirit over all flesh,
and your sons and your daughters will prophesy,
and your youths will see visions,
and your elders will dream dreams,
and assuredly over my slaves
and over my handmaids in those days,
I will pour out from my Spirit and they will prophesy.
And in Hosea He says, I will call 'not my folk' 'my folk',

and 'not having acquired pity' 'having acquired pity',

and there will be in the place where 'you [are] not my folk' was said,
there they will be called sons of the living God.
Whence moreover in Ireland those who never had notice of God,

nisi idola . et inmunda usque nunc sémper coluérunt .

60   Quomodo 'nuper facta est plebs Domini'.
et filii Déi nuncupántur
filii Scottorum . et filiae règulórum .
monachi et uirgines Xpisti ésse uidéntur .

(42)   Et etiam una benedicta Scotta genetíua **n**óbilis
65   pulcherrima adúlta érat .
quam égo báptizáui .
Et post paucos dies una caúsa uénit ád nos .
insinuauit nobis responsum accepisse a núntio Déi .

et monuit eam ut ésset uírgo Xpísti .
70   et ipsa Déo proximáret .
Déo grátias
sexta ab hac die optime et auidissime **a**rrípuit **í**llud .
quod etiam omnes uirgines Dei íta hoc fáciunt .
non sponte pátrum eárum .
75   sed et persecutiónes patiúntur
et improperia falsa a paréntibus súis .
et nihilominus plus augétur númerus .
et de genere nostro qui íbi náti sunt
nescimus númerum eórum .
80   praeter uiduas et cóntinéntes .
Sed et illae maxime laborant quae seruítio dètinéntur .
usque ad terrores et minas assídue . pérferunt .
Sed Dominus gratiam dedit multis ex ancíllis súis .
Nam etsi uetantur . tamen fórtiter ìmitántur .

(43)6   1   Unde autem etsi uoluero **a**míttere íllas .
et ut pérgens in Brittánniis
     2   et libentissime 'paratus eram'.
quasi ad pátriam èt paréntes .
Non id solum .
90   sed etiam usque ad Gallias uísitáre frátres .
       a   et ut uiderem faciem sanctorum *Dómini* méi .
     b   i   **S**cit Deus quod *ego* uálde optábam .
   3   ii   *sed 'alligatus Spiritu'*
      iii   *qui mihi 'protestatur' . sí hoc fécero .*
95   iv   *ut futurum reum me ésse désignat .*
      c   *et timeo perdere laborem quém inchoáui .*
    b'   i   **E**t non *ego*
      ii   *sed Xpístus Dóminus*
      iii   *qui mé imperáuit*

up to now they always worshipped nothing except idols and unclean things,
how recently a folk of the Lord has been made,
and they are named sons of God.
The sons and daughters of the petty kings of the Scots
are seen to be monks and virgins of Christ,
and there was even one blessed Scotswoman, noble from birth,
most beautiful as a grown woman,
whom I baptized,
and after a few days for one cause she came to us,
she made known to us that she had received an answer from a messenger
   of God,
and he monished her that she should be a virgin of Christ,
and that she should draw near to God.
Thanks be to God,
on the sixth day from this she most excellently and most eagerly accepted that,
because all virgins of God do this even so,
not with the willing assent of their fathers,
but they even suffer persecutions
and false reproaches from their own parents,
and nonetheless their number is increased more,
and those who have been born from our begetting,
we do not know their number,
besides widows and continent women.
But they also labour most who are detained in service;
they bear continually [everything] up to the point of terrors and threats,
but the Lord has given grace to many of His own handmaids,
for even if they are forbidden, nevertheless they imitate this conduct
   vigorously.

Whence moreover even if I should have wished to lose them,
so that proceeding even to the Britains,
and most willingly I was prepared,
as if to fatherland and parents,
not only that,
but even as far as the Gauls to visit brothers,
and that I might see the face of the holy men of my Lord.
God knows what I preferred especially,
but bound by the Spirit,
Who protests to me if I shall have done this,
that He marks me out to be guilty for the future,
and I fear to lose the labour which I have begun,
and not I,
but Christ the Lord
Who has commanded me

100   iv   *ut uenirem . esse cum illis residuum aetátis méae .*

    a'   'si *Dominus* uoluerit'.

         et custodierit me ab ómni uía mála

         ut non 'peccem coram illo'.

(44) 7   <u>Spero autem hóc debúeram</u> .

105   sed memet ípsum nón credo .

         'quamdiu fuero in hoc corpore mortis'.

    a   *quia fortis est qui cotidie nititur subuértere mè a fide .*

    b   *et praeposita castitate religiónis non fictae .*

    cd   USQUE IN FINEM UITAE MEAE Xpisto *Dómino méo .*

110   e   **Sed** *'caro inimica' semper tráhit ad mórtem .*

    f   **Id** *est* **ad** *inlecebras inlicitate pérficiéndas .*

    e'   **Et** *'scio ex parte' quare uitam perfectam égo non égi .*

         'sicut' et 'céteri' credéntes .

    d'   **Sed** confiteor *Dómino méo*

115   et non erubesco in conspéctu ípsius .

         'QUIA NON MENTIOR'.

    c'   ex quo cognoui eum *'a iuuentute mea'* .

    b'   *creuit in me* **a**mor *Dei et tímor ípsius .*

    a'   *'et usque nunc' fauente Domino 'fidem seruaui'.*

(45)   **R**ideat **a**utem et insúltet qui uolúerit .

         ego non silebo neque abscondo signa et mírabília

         quae mihi a Dómino monstráta sunt .

         Ante multos ánnos . quam fierent .

         quasi qui nouit omnia etiam '**a**nte tempora saecularia'.

(46)6'1 ab   <u>Unde autem debueram</u> sine cessatione Deo *grátias* ágere .

    c   qui saepe indulsit *insipiéntiae méae .*

         neglegéntiae méae .

         et de loco nón in úno quóque .

         ut non mihi ueheménter iràscerétur .

130   qui ádiutor dátus sum .

         et non cito adquieui secundum quod mihi osténsum fúerat .

    3   **E**t sicut 'Spiritus sugge<u>rebat</u>'.

         et 'misertus est' mihi Dominus 'in milia milium'.

    2   d   *quia uidit in me quod 'paratus eram'* .

135   d'   *sed quod mihi pro hís nesciébam .*

         de statu méo quid fácerem .

         quia multi hanc legatiónem prohibébant .

         etiam inter se ipsos post tergum méum narrábant

         et dicebant . "**I**ste quare se mittit ín perículo

140   inter hostes qui Déum nón nouérunt ?"

that I should come to be with them for the rest of my lifetime,
if the Lord will have wished,
and He will have kept watch over me from every bad way,
so that I do not sin before Him.

I hope moreover that I ought [or 'was bound' to do] this,
but I do not believe in myself,
for as long as I will have been in this body of death,
because he is vigorous, he who strives daily to subvert me from the faith
and from the chastity of a religion not feigned set before [me],
up to the end of my life for Christ my Lord.
But the inimical flesh always drags toward death,
that is, toward allurements to be dealt with illicitly,
and I know in part why I have not lived a perfect life,
just as the others also believing,
but I confess to my Lord,
and I do not blush for shame in His sight,
as I do not lie,
because I have known Him from my youth,
in me the love of God and fear of Him has grown,
and up to now, with the Lord favouring, I have kept the faith.
Let him who will have wished moreover laugh and insult,
I shall not be silent, nor do I hide signs and wonders,
which have been shown to me by the Lord
many years before they may be made,
as He Who knows all things even before the times of the ages.

Whence moreover I ought [or 'was bound'] to give thanks without ceasing
    to God,
Who has often conceded to my unwisdom,
to my carelessness,
even out of place, not on one [occasion] either,
that He would not grow vehemently angry with me,
who have been given as a helper,
and I did not acquiesce quickly according to what had been shown to me,
and just as the Spirit was suggesting to me,
the Lord has shown pity to me up to thousands of thousands of times,
because He saw in me that I was ready,
but that I did not know for myself for these circumstances,
what I should do about my own condition,
because many were hindering this embassy.
They were even talking among themselves behind my back
and saying, "Why does this man dispatch himself in peril
among enemies who do not know God?"

Non ut caúsa malítiae .
sed nón sapièbat íllis .
sicut et égo ípse téstor

    c'   intellegi propter *rustícitátem méam* .
145 b'   et non cito **a**gnoui *gratiam* quae túnc erat ín me .
    a'   Nunc mihi sapit *quod ánte debúeram* .

(47) 5'   Nunc ergo simpliciter insinuaui fratribus ét cónséruis méis .
qui mihi crediderunt . propter quod 'praedixi et praedico'

ad roborandum et confirmándam fidem uéstram .
150   Utinam ut et uos imitemini maiora et potióra faciátis .

Hoc erit glória méa .
quia 'filius sapiens .
gloria patris est'.
(48)   Uos scitis et Deus qualiter inter uos cónuersátus sum
155   'A iuuentute mea'.
in fide ueritatis 'et in sinceritate cordis'.
Etiam ad gentes illas ínter quas hábito .
ego fidem illis praestáui . et praestábo .

Deus scit 'neminem' illórum 'circumuéni'.
160   nec cogito propter Deum et ecclésiam ípsius .
ne 'excitem' illis et nobis omnibus 'persecutionem'.
et ne per me blasphemaretur nómen Dómini .
quia scriptum est . 'Uae homini
per quem nomen Domini blasphematur'.
(49)   Nam 'etsi imperitus sum . **i**n omnibus'.
tamen conatus sum quíppiam seruáre me .
etiam et frátribus Xpìstiánis
et uirginibus Xpisti . et mulieribus relígiósis
quae mihi ultronea munúscula donábant .
170   et super altare iactabant . ex órnaméntis súis .
et iterum reddébam íllis .
et aduersus me scandalizabantur . cur hóc faciébam .

    4'   Sed ego propter spém perennitátis .
ut me in omnibus caute proptérea cònseruárem .
175   ita ut non me in aliquo titulo infidéli cáperent .
uel ministerium . séruitútis méae .
nec etiam in minimo incredulis locum darem . infamare
    síue detractáre .
(50) 1   Forte autem quando baptizaui tot mília hóminum .

Not as from a cause of malice,
but it did not seem wise to them,
just as I myself bear witness,
to be understood on account of my rusticity,
and not quickly did I acknowledge the grace which was then in me.
Now what I ought [to have done] before seems wise to me.

Now therefore I have simply made known to my brothers and fellow slaves,
who have believed in me on account of what I have said beforehand and
    proclaim,
for corroborating and confirming your faith.
Would that you also imitate the greater things and perform more powerful
    things.
This will be my glory,
because a wise son
is the glory of a father.
You know, God also, how I have conducted myself among you
from my youth
in the faith of truth and in sincerity of heart.
Even to these gentiles among whom I dwell
I have supplied and I will supply faith to them [*i.e.* 'I have kept and I will
    keep my word to them'].
God knows I have cheated [lit. 'gone round'] none of them,
nor do I think, on account of God and His Church,
that I would rouse up persecution for them and all of us,
nor that the name of the Lord should be blasphemed through me,
because it is written, Woe to the man
through whom the name of the Lord is blasphemed.
For even if I am unlearned in all things,
nevertheless I have tried to some degree to save myself,
even also for Christian brothers
and virgins of Christ and religious women,
who kept giving me voluntary little gifts,
and they kept hurling some of their own ornaments over the altar,
and I kept giving them back again to them,
and they kept being scandalized in response to me because I kept doing this.

But I on account of the hope of everlastingness,
so that I would preserve myself cautiously in all things on that account,
so that they would not on any legal charge of unfaithfulness capture me
or the ministry of my slavery,
nor would I give a place even in the least degree to unbelievers to defame
    or detract.
Perhaps moreover when I baptized so many thousands of men

sperauerim ab aliquo illorum uel dimídio scríptulae .

180	'Dicite mihi . et reddam uobis'.
2	Aut quando ordinauit ubique Dóminus cléricos
	per modicitatem meam . et ministerium . gratis
	distríbui íllis .
	si poposci ab aliquo illorum . uel pretium uel
	'cálciamènti' méi .
	'dicite aduersus me . et réddam uobis' mágis .
(51)	Ego 'impendi pro' uóbis ut me 'cáperent'.
	et inter uos et ubique pergebam causa uestra in múltis
	perículis
3	etiam usque ad éxteras pártes .
	ubi némo últra érat .
	et ubi numquam áliquis peruénerat .
190 1'	qui báptizáret .
2'	aut cléricos òrdináret .
1"	aut pópulum cònsummáret .
	Donánte Dómino
	diligenter et líbentíssime
195	pro salute uestra ómnia gèneráui .
(52) 3'	Interim praemia dábam régibus .
	praeter quod dabam mercedem filiis ipsórum
	qui mécum ámbulant .
	et nihilominus comprehenderunt me cum comítibus méis .
200	Et illa die auidissime cupiebant interficere me [? l. mé
	interficere] .
	Sed tempus nóndum uénerat .
	Et omnia quaecumque nobiscum inuenerunt rápuérunt .
	íllud .
	et me ipsum férro uinxérunt .
	Et quartodecimo die absoluit me Dominus de potestáte
	eórum .
205	et quicquid nostrum fuit redditum est nóbis . propter Déum
	et 'necessarios amicos' quos ánte praeuídimus .
(53)	Uos aútem expèrti éstis
	quantum ego érogáui íllis .
	qui iudicabant 'per omnes regiones'.
210	quos ego frequéntius uìsitábam .
	Censeo enim non minimum quam pretium quindecim
	hominum distríbui íllis .
	ita ut mé 'fruámini' .
	et ego 'uobis' semper 'frúar' in Déum .
	Nón me paénitet .

I would have hoped for even half a scruple [*i.e.* 1/576th of a unit] from
   any of them.
Tell me, and I will give it back to you.
Or when the Lord ordained clerics everywhere
through my littleness and I distributed the ministry to them free,

if I asked for even the price even of my shoe from any of them,

tell it to my face and I will give more back to you.
I have spent for you that they might receive [lit. 'capture'] me,
and among you and everywhere I proceeded in your cause in many perils,

even as far as remote parts,
where there was no man beyond,
and where no one had ever come through,
who would baptize
or ordain clerics
or bring the people to the highest perfection.
With the Lord granting,
with loving care and most willingly,
I have begotten all things for your salvation.

Meanwhile I kept giving rewards to kings,
besides which I kept giving a fee to their sons,
who walk with me,
and nonetheless they apprehended me with my companions,
and on that day they wanted most eagerly to kill me,

but the time had not yet come,
and all things whatsoever they discovered [lit. 'came upon'] with us, they
   seized it,
and fettered myself with iron,
and on the fourteenth day the Lord released me from their power,

and whatsoever was ours was given back to us on account of God,
and close friends whom we saw to before.
You furthermore have proved by experience
how much I have paid out to those
who judged [*i.e.* the brehons] through all the regions
which I kept visiting quite often.
For I reckon that I have distributed to them not less than the price of
   fifteen men
so that you might enjoy me,
and I will always enjoy you in God.
It does not cause me regret

215   nec sátis est míhi .
                         adhuc 'impendo et superimpendam' .
      2'   **P**otens est Dominus ut det míhi póstmodum .
218 1'   ut meipsum 'impendar pro animabus uestris'.

PART **V**

(54) XXI F'
  1   a   i   **E**cce *'testem Deum inuoco* in animam meam .
  2   ii   QUIA NON MENTIOR' .
                         neque ut sit 'occasio **a**dulationis'
                         uel 'auaritiae' scrípserim uóbis .
  5   b   *neque ut* HONOREM *spero* ab áliquo uéstro .
      b'   **S**u*fficit enim* HONOR qui nondum uidetur . sed córde
                           créditur .
      a' i   '*Fidelis*' autem '*qui promisit* .
          ii   *numquam* MENTITUR' .

(55) XXII E'
                         Sed uideo iam 'in praesenti saeculo'
                         me supra modum exaltátum a Dómino .
  1   et non eram dígnus neque tális
                         ut hoc míhi praestáret .
  5   dum scío certíssime
                         quod mihi melius conuenit paupertas . ét calámitas .

                         quam diuitiae ét dilíciae .
                         Sed et Xpistus Dominus pauper' fúit 'pro nóbis'.
                         Ego uero míser et ínfelix .
  10   **E**tsi opes uoluero iám non hábeo .
                         'neque me ipsum iudico'.
                         quia cotídie spéro
                         aut internicionem . aut círcumueníri .
                         aut redigi in seruitutem . siue occásio cuiúslibet .
  15   '**S**ed nihil horum uereor' . propter promíssa caelórum .

                         quia iactaui meipsum in manus Dei ómnipoténtis .
                         qui úbique dòminátur.

      XXIII D'
                         Sícut prophèta dícit .
                         '**I**acta cogitatum tuum in Deum .
                         et ipse te enutriet' .
  (56)   **E**cce nunc 'commendo animam meam fidelíssimo
                           Dèo' méo .
  5   'pro quo legationem fungor' **i**n ignobílitáte méa .
                         Sed quia 'personam non accipit'.

nor is it enough to me
that I spend and I shall overspend farther.
The Lord is powerful that He may give me afterward,
that I may spend myself for your souls.

PART V

Look, I call on God as testifier for my soul
that I do not lie.
Neither that it be an occasion of flattery
or of avarice that I shall have written to you,
nor that I hope for honour from any of you,
for honour suffices which is not yet seen but is believed in the heart.

He moreover is faithful Who has promised,
He never lies.

But I see now in the present age
myself exalted by the Lord beyond measure,
and I was not worthy nor such
that He should supply this to me,
while I know most certainly,
that poverty and calamity has been convenient [lit. 'come together'], better
    for me
than riches and delights.
But Christ the Lord was also poor for us,
for I, pitiable and unhappy,
even if I will have wished, I do not now have resources,
nor do I judge myself,
because I hope daily
either massacre or being cheated [lit. 'gone round']
or led back into slavery or an occasion of some sort.
But I am in awe of none of these things on account of the promises of the
    heavens,
because I have hurled myself into the hands of all-powerful God,
Who rules as lord everywhere.

Just as the prophet says,
Hurl your thought on God,
and He will nourish you.
Look, now I commend my soul to my most faithful God,

for Whom I perform an embassy in my ignobility,
but as He does not receive theatrical impersonation,

　　　　　　et elegit mé ad hoc officium
　　　　　　ut 'unus'. essem 'de suis mínimis'. mínister .

(57) XXIIII C'

　　　　　　Unde autem 'retribuam illi .
　　　　　　pro omnibus quae retribuit mihi'?
　　　　　　Sed quid dicam .
　　　　　　uel quid promittam Dómino méo ?
5　　　　　　quia níhil uáleo
　　　　　　nisi ipse míhi déderit .
　　　　　　Sed 'scrutatur corda . et renes'.
　　　　　　quia satis et nimis cupio . et 'paratus eram'
　　　　　　ut donaret mihi 'bibere cálicem' eíus .
10　　　　　sicut indulsit et ceteris amantibus se [? l. sé amántibus] .
(58)　　　　Quapropter non contingat míhi a Dèo méo .
　　　　　　ut numquam amíttam 'plebem' súam .
　　　　　　'quam adquisiuit' in últimis térrae .
　　　　　　Oro Deum ut det mihi pérseuerántiam .
15　　　　　et dignetur ut reddam illi téstem fidélem .
　　　　　　usque ad transitum meum própter Déum méum .
(59)　　　　Et si aliquid boni úmquam imitátus sum
　　　　　　propter Deum méum quem díligo .
　　　　　　Peto ílli det míhi
20　　　　　ut cum illis proselitis et captiuis pro nómine súo
　　　　　　effundam sánguinem méum .
　　　　　　etsi ipsam etiam cáream sèpultúram
　　　　　　Aut miserissime cadauer per singula membra diuidátur
　　　　　　　　cánibus .
　　　　　　aut béstiis ásperis
25　　　　　Aut 'uolucres caeli comederent illud'.
　　　　　　Certíssime réor .
　　　　　　si mihi hóc incurrísset
　　　　　　lucratus sum animam cum córpore méo .
　　　　　　quia 'sine ulla dubitatione' in die illa 'resurgemus' in
　　　　　　　　cláritáte sólis .
30　　　　　Hoc est 'in gloria' Xpisti Iesu redémptoris nóstri .
　　　　　　quasi 'filii Dei' uiui et 'coheredes Xpisti' .
　　　　　　et 'conformes futuri imaginis ipsius'.
　　　　　　Quoniam 'ex ipso . et per ipsum . et in ipso' régnatúri
　　　　　　　　súmus .
(60)　　　　Nam sol iste quem uidemus . ipso iubente propter nos
　　　　　　　　cotídie óritur .
35　　　　　sed numquam regnabit neque permanébit splendor eíus .
　　　　　　Sed et omnes qui adorant eum . in poenam miseri mále
　　　　　　　　deuénient .

He chose even me for this office,
that I should be one minister from among His own least.

Whence moreover shall I hand back to Him
for all the things which He has handed back to me?
But what shall I say,
or what shall I promise to my Lord,
as I can do nothing
unless Himself will have given to me,
but He examines the hearts and reins,
as enough and too much I want, and I was ready
that He should grant to me to drink His chalice,
just as He conceded also to others loving Him.
On which account it should not befall to me from my God
that I should ever lose His own folk
which He has acquired in the furthest parts of land.
I pray God that He may give me perseverance
and deign that I shall give back to Him a faithful testifier
up to the point of my passing over on account of my God.
And if I have ever imitated anything of the good
on account of my God whom I love dearly,
I seek from Him that He give to me
that with those sojourners and captives for His own name
I should pour out my blood,
even if I should lack even burial itself,
or my cadaver be most pitiably divided by single members for dogs

or for savage beasts
or birds of heaven should eat it up.
Most certainly I consider,
if this should happen to me,
I have gained the soul as profit with my body,
because without any doubt on that day we shall rise again in the brightness
    of the sun,
this is, in the glory of Christ Jesus our Redeemer,
as sons of the living God and fellow heirs of Christ,
and going to be conformed to His image,
since from Him and through Him and in Him we are going to reign.

For this sun which we see rises daily on our account, with Himself order-
    ing it,
but it will never reign, nor will its splendour remain forever,
but even all who adore it will come badly to the punishment of the
    pitiable.

Nos autem qui credimus et adoramus sólem uerum
    Xpístum
qui númquam interíbit .
neque 'qui fecerit uoluntátem' ípsius .

40   Sed 'manebit in aeternum .
Quomodo et Xpistus manet in aeternum'
qui regnat cum Deo Patre ómnipoténte .
et cum Spiritu Sancto ánte saécula
et nunc et per omnia saécula saèculórum Amen .

(61) XXV B'

1   Ecce iterum iterumque breuiter exponam uerba
    Conféssiónis méae .

3   'Testificor' in ueritate et in 'exultatione cordis coram
    Deo et sanctis angelis eius' .
quia numquam habui aliquam occásiónem
praeter éuangélium

5   et promíssa íllius

2   ut umquam redírem ad gèntem íllam .
Unde prius uíx euáseram.

(62)XXVI A'

Sed précor credéntibus .
et timéntibus Déum
Quicumque dignatus fúerit inspícere
uel recípere hànc scriptúram .

5 1 2 3   quam Patricius peccator . indoctus scilicet HIBERIÓNE
    conscrípsit .

4   ut nemo umquam dicat quod mea ígnorántia .
Si aliquid PUSILLUM . egi uel démonstráuerim
secundum Déi plácitum .
Sed arbitramini et ueríssime credátur

10   quod 'donum Déi' fuísset .
ET haec est Conféssio méa
ÁNTEQUAM MÓRIAR :;

We moreover who believe and adore the true sun Christ,

Who will never die,
nor he who will have done His will,
but he will remain for eternity,
in the same fashion as Christ also remains for eternity,
Who reigns with God the Father all-powerful,
and with the Holy Spirit before the ages,
and now and through all ages of ages. Amen.

Look, again and again briefly I will set out the words of my Confession.

I bear testimony in truth and in exultation of heart before God and His
    holy angels
that I have never had any occasion
besides the Gospel
and His promises
that I should ever go back to that gentile people
whence earlier I had barely escaped.

But I beseech those believing
and fearing God,
whoever will have deigned to look on
or receive this writing,
which Patrick, a sinner, untaught, to be sure, wrote down in Ireland,

that no man should ever say that by my ignorance,
if I have accomplished or demonstrated any small thing
according to the acceptable purpose of God,
but that you judge and it must be most truly believed
that it was the gift of God,
and this is my Confession
before I die.

CONFESSIO

ANALYSIS AND COMMENTARY

Let us begin by establishing the limits of the chapter divisions of part **I** and part **V** and their parallel and chiastic links. The *Confessio* begins with a Prologue, chapter I (1-2) A, which exhibits internal chiasmus. Compare ai *ego* 1 with a'i *me* 28, aii *patrem* 4 with a'ii *pater* 28, aiii *filium* 5 with a'iii *filium* 28. Patrick refers to his age in bi *annorum eram tunc fere sedecim* 9 and b'i *adolescentiae* 24, to God in bii *Deum* 10 and b'ii *Deum* 22, to his ignorance in biii *ignorabam* 10 and b'iii *ignorantiae meae* 24, to his abject lowliness in captivity in biv *Hiberione in captiuitate adductus sum* 11 and b'iv *humilitatem meam* 23. He uses in bv the verb *custodiuimus* 14 and in b'v the verb *custodiuit* 25. He contrasts disobedience to the counsel of priests for salvation in c *et sacerdotibus nostris non oboedientes fuimus qui nostram salutem admonebant* 15-6 with the first step toward salvation in c' *ut uel sero rememorarem delicta mea* 21. At the crux he mentions punishment from the Lord in di *et Dominus induxit super nos iram animationis suae* 17 and the beginning of understanding from the Lord in di' *et ibi Dominus aperuit sensum incredulitatis meae* 20 and the exile which issued from the former in dii *et dispersit nos in gentibus multis etiam usque ad ultimum terrae* 18 and led to the latter in dii' *ubi nunc paruitas mea esse uidetur inter alienigenas* 19. The twenty-eight lines of chapter I divide by extreme and mean ratio at 17 and 11. The seventeenth line is the beginning of the crux at di. The 149 words of chapter I divide by symmetry at the central seventy-fifth word, *ET* at the beginning of the crux at di. There are capital letters at the beginnings of di *ET* 17 and di' *ET* 20 and *puncti eleuati* at the ends of line 16, just before the beginning of the crux, and line 18, exactly at the crux.

The *Confessio* ends with an Epilogue, chapter XXVI (62) A', which Patrick has linked to the Prologue. Compare *Patricius peccator* 1, *Hiberione* 11, *ignorantiae meae* 24 in A with *Patricius peccator* 5, *Hiberione* 5, *mea ignorantia* 6 in A'. These are the only two places in the entire work in which Patrick mentions his name and uses the nouns *peccator* and *ignorantia*.

In chapter II (3) B he states his reason for writing: *unde autem tacere non possum*; he describes Ireland as *terra captiuitatis meae*; and he echoes Psalm LXXXVIII 6: *exaltare et confiteri mirabilia eius*. Similarly in chapter XXV (61) B' he restates his reason for writing: *ecce iterum iterumque breuiter exponam uerba Confessionis meae*; he describes the Irish as *gentem illam unde prius uix euaseram*; and he echoes Psalm CXVIII 111: *testificor in exultatione cordis coram Deo et sanctis angelis eius*.

Chapter III (4) C Patrick devotes to a Creed of thirty-three lines and 144 words. Comparably he devotes chapter XXIIII (57-60) C' to a Doxology of forty-four lines and 265 words. The thirty-first line of the former mentions *filii Dei et coheredes Xpisti;* the thirty-first line of the latter mentions *filii Dei uiui et coheredes Xpisti,* both echoing Romans VIII 16-7, a text quoted only here.

Compare chapter IIII (5) D with chapter XXIII (55 end – 56) D'. In the former Patrick writes *ipse enim dixit per prophetam;* in the latter he writes *sicut propheta dicit.* In the former he quotes Psalm XLIX 15; in the latter he quotes Psalm LIV 23. In both chapters the prophet referred to is David as author of the entire Psalter. Chapter IIII contains twenty-eight words and chapter XXIII forty-five, together seventy-three words, which divide by extreme and mean ratio at 45 and 28.

Patrick confesses his unworthiness in chapters V (6) E, *in multis imperfectus sum,* and XXII (55) E', *non eram dignus neque talis ut hoc mihi praestaret.*

In chapter XXI (54) F' Patrick arranged his ideas in a little chiasmus, balancing ai *testem Deum inuoco* with a'i *fidelis ... qui promisit* [*sc. Deus*], and aii *quia non mentior* with a'ii *numquam mentitur,* around the crux at b *neque ut honorem spero* and b' *sufficit enim honor.* The forty-one words divide by symmetry at 21, which divides by extreme and mean ratio at 13 and 8. There are thirteen words from *mentior* to *honorem* inclusive. There are eight words from *honorem* to *honor* inclusive. There are thirteen words from *honor* to *mentitur* inclusive. The pair to this is chapter VI (7) F, in which Patrick writes *non ignoro testimonium Domini mei* and *os quod mentitur occidit animam.*

The six chapters I-VI (1-8) which begin part **I** of the *Confessio* contain ninety-six lines of text. The six chapters XXI-XXVI (54-62) which end the *Confessio* in part **V** also contain ninety-six lines of text.

Part **I** ends with Patrick's Apology, chapter VII (9-15), which, uniquely, has no chiastic pair in the *Confessio,* but is itself chiastically composed within the limits of the *inclusio* marked by the verb *cogitaui* in the first line and as the last word. Let us examine first the balance of words and phrases. Patrick feared the censure of learned men's tongues, *ne inciderem in linguam hominum* 3, because he had not learned, *non didici* 4, unlike those who *iura . . . combiberunt* 5-6 in 1b. Yet God from the midst of them roused up, *excitauit de medio eorum* 61, the unlearned Patrick, *me stultum* 61, unlike those *legis periti* 62, in 1'b. Compare *sermones* 7 in 1c with *in sermone* 63 in 1'c and *translata est* 9 in 1d with *transtulit* 68 in 1'd. Note also the reference in 1d to the Irish language, *in linguam alienam* 9 and the two references in 1'd to Irish people, *genti* 67 and *in gentem illam* 83. The passage marked 1'd is remarkable for internal chiasmus, *et . . . si talis essem* 64-5 in ia echoed by *et non eram . . . talis* 79 in i'a, *ut . . . genti* 66-7 in ib echoed by *ut . . . in gentem illam* 80-3 in i'b, *donauit me* 69 in ic echoed by *mihi donaret* 84 in i'c. Compare *ut . . . deseruirem illis* 70 in ii with *ut . . . exagallias relinquere fratribus et filiis meis* 77 in ii', *sine reprehensione periculi* 72 in iiia with *sine timore* 75 in iii'a and *notum facere* and *donum Dei* 73 in iiib with *ubique*

expandere and *Dei nomen* 76 in iii'b. Note *in iuuentute non comparaui* 17 in
1e, echoed by *in iuuentute . . . numquam speraui* 85 in 1'e.

In the passage I have marked 1 Bieler noted nine clausulae.[19] I note
eighteen, inferring that Patrick intended every line except the Biblical
quotation at the end of 1d to end with a clausula. He may even have made
chiastic patterns of clausular types. Among the first seven compare the first, a
molossus–iamb, with the seventh, a molossus–spondee; the second with the
sixth, both cretic–double trochees; the third with the fifth, each a molossus-
iamb; around the fourth and central double cretic; making a pattern A-B-A-
C-A-B-A'. Among the second six compare the first half-clausula, a trochaic
metron 8, with the lack of a clausula in the Biblical quotation 12-3; the
second 9, a molossus–double trochee, with the fourth 11, a cretic–double
trochee, around the third and central molossus–iamb 10; making a pattern X'-
B'-A-B-XX. Among the last seven are two examples of molossus–double
trochee 14-5; two examples of cretic–double trochee 16-7 (with one false
quantity in *mea* 16); a molossus–spondee 18; a double cretic 19; and a
cretic–molossus 20; making a pattern B'-B'-B-B-A'C-C'.

Patrick describes himself as *paene ... inuerbis* 'almost wordless' 21 in 2a
and as *primus rusticus* 'the extreme rustic' 44 and *indoctus* 'untaught' 45 in
2'a-b, perhaps alluding both times to his lack of formal education in
rhetoric. He describes himself as a captive 22 in 2b and as an exile 45 in
2'b. Compare *antequam scirem quid adpetere* 23 in 2c with *priusquam, nescio*
and *scio*, and *prouidere* 46-47 in 2'c, and *non silerem propter retributionem* 32 in
2e with *debueram exclamare ad retribuendum* 53-4 in 2'e.

Let us examine next Patrick's use of Biblical quotations. In 1a the words
usque nunc 2 may derive from Mark XIII 19, 'the Little Apocalypse', in which
Jesus foretells 'the desolating sacrilege set up where it ought not to be', when
'false Christs and false prophets will arise'. Mark writes *erunt enim dies illi
tribulationes tales quales non fuerunt . . . usque nunc . . . sed propter electos quos
elegit breuiauit dies.* With this compare the quotation from the Apocalypse XIX
5 in 1'a, *qui timetis eum pusilli et magni* 58, part of a little chiasmus:

   i   **U**nde autem admiramini itaque
   ii   magni et pusilli
   iii   qui timetis
   iv   Deum .
   iii'   et uos
   ii'   domini cati rethorici .
   i'   **A**udite ergo et scrutamini

The chiastic structure implies that the *domini cati rethorici* are not included
among the great and small who fear God. The quotation comes from the

19 Bieler, *Libri* XII 113.

centre of a passage which contrasts the fall of the harlot Babylon the great, in which the blood of prophets and saints has been found, with the preparation of the chaste Bride for marriage to the Lamb. One infers from these unquoted contexts that Patrick has been compelled to write at a time of tribulation and that his critics are among the *pseudochristi* and *pseudoprophetae*, those in Babylon who attack prophets and saints, while he is one of the *electi* with the Bride. In 1b the words *ne inciderem in linguam* 3 allude to Ecclesiasticus XXVIII 23-7, *beatus qui tectus est a lingua nequa . . . qui derelinquunt Deum incident in illam.* One infers from the unquoted context that Patrick is *beatus* and *tectus* and that he will not abandon God. The words *sicut ceteri* 4 come from I Thessalonians V 6, where 'the others' are not Christians. In 1c the words *ad perfectum* 8 come from Hebrews VII 19, *nihil enim ad perfectum adduxit lex*, implying that the learning of 'the others' has not brought them the perfection which on a first reading Patrick might seem to concede to them.[20] Similarly in 1'c one reads of the learned as *potentes in sermone* 63, echoing the description in Luke XXIV 19 of Jesus, *qui fuit uir . . . potens in . . . sermone*. But this is feint praise. Those whom Patrick describes only *uidentur esse* 62 'seem to be wise and learned by experience in law and powerful in speech and in everything'. In 1d the phrase *sermo et loquela* 9 has two sources. The first is Psalm XVIII 4-5:

> non sunt loquellae neque sermones
> quorum non audiantur uoces eorum
> in omnem terram exiuit sonus eorum
> et in fines orbis terrae uerba eorum.

The second is John VIII 43-4:

> quare loquellam meam non cognoscitis
> quia non potestis audire sermonem meum
> uos ex patre diabolo estis.

The former is consistent with Patrick's enforced speaking of Old Irish at the ends of the earth; the latter implies again that his critics are not on the side of the angels. In the quotation from Ecclesiasticus IV 29 at the end of 1d 12-3 Patrick has changed *sapientia* to *sapiens*. According to Bieler, 'Patrick's quotation, apparently made from memory, is not quite exact . . . . It may thus be permissible to assume that Patrick — unconsciously — replaced *sapientia* by *sapiens*.'[21] Not, I think, unconsciously. As the quotation directly follows a clause referring to his own education the inescapable inference is that Patrick is claiming to be *sapiens*. In 1d-e he has surrounded this quotation

20 This corroborates Bieler's suggestion, *Libri* XII 112, that enclitic *itaque* 'seems to give *optime* an ironical undertone'.
21 Bieler, *Libri* XII 116.

with echoes of Acts XXII 3, in which St Paul, addressing a hostile mob in their own language, says, *ego sum . . . nutritus autem . . . secus pedes Gamalihel, eruditus iuxta ueritatem paternae legis*. Also in 1e 16–7 is an echo of Ecclesiasticus XXV 5, *in iuuentute tua non congregasti et quomodo inuenies eam in senectute tua?* The passage in 1'di is studded with quotations, mostly Pauline. Note the contexts. The phrase *cum metu et reuerentia* 66 comes from Hebrews XII 28, *habemus gratiam per quam seruiamus placentes Deo cum metu et reuerentia*. The phrase *sine querella* occurs three times in I Thessalonians II 10, III 13, and V 23:

> memores enim estis fratres laborem nostrum et fatigationem
> nocte et die operantes ne quem uestrum grauaremus
> praedicauimus in uobis euangelium Dei
> uos testes estis et Deus
> quam sancte et iuste et sine querella uobis qui credidistis fuimus
> sicut scitis
> qualiter unumquemque uestrum tamquam pater filios suos
> deprecantes uos et consolantes testificati sumus ... .
> nocte et die abundantius orantes ...
> ad confirmanda corda uestra sine querella in sanctitate ...
> integer spiritus uester
> et anima et corpus
> sine querella in aduentu Domini nostri Iesu Christi seruetur.

The phrase *caritas Xpisti* comes from II Corinthians V 14:

> non iterum nos commendamus uobis
> sed occasionem damus uobis gloriandi pro nobis ...
> caritas enim Christi urget nos.

From the first of these contexts one infers that Patrick is implicitly claiming that he has *gratiam* and that he is *placens Deo*. The second lists Paul's heroic efforts for his converts. The third claims that the love of Christ is working for His Apostle's converts. Note in the parallel passage i'b the list of Patrick's heroic efforts for his converts and his explicit claim to *gratiam*. The phrase *mensura fidei* in iiia comes from Romans XII 3, *Deus diuisit mensuram fidei*. The words *donum Dei* in iiib come from John IV 10. At the centre in iv *consolationem aeternam* comes from II Thessalonians II 16. And the phrase *post obitum meum* in ii' comes from II Peter I 15.

In paragraphs 2 and 2' Patrick apparently admits ignorance. In 2d 28 he quotes Ecclesiastes I 8, *cunctae res difficiles non potest eas homo explicare sermone*. Again in 2'c 46 he quotes Ecclesiastes IV 13:

> melior est puer pauper et sapiens rege sene et stulto

> qui nescit prouidere in posterum
> quod et de carcere catenisque interdum quis egrediatur ad regnum.

The context, which he does not quote, links this passage backward to the parallel paragraph 2, in which he is a *puer* in a, a captive figuratively at least *in carcere catenisque* in b, not yet *sapiens* in c. It also links this passage forward to paragraph 1'b, in which Patrick describes himself as *stultum*. But the principal function of the quotation is to point a contrast to the immediately following clauses, in which he says what he does know certainly. Here he quotes I Samuel XXIV 21, *et nunc quia scio quod certissime regnaturus sis*. Saul is speaking to David, who will one day be the Lord's Anointed. In the next clause by an easy association Patrick quotes David's Psalm CXVIII 67, *priusquam humiliarer ego deliqui propterea eloquium tuum custodiui*, and in the next clause Psalm LXVIII 15:

> eripe me de luto ut non infigar
> liberer ab his qui oderunt me
> et de profundis aquarum.

In 2'd he quotes the Magnificat from Luke I 49-54:

> quia fecit mihi magna qui potens est ...
> et misericordia eius in progenies ...
> deposuit potentes de sede et exaltauit humiles ...
> suscepit Israhel puerum suum memorari misericordiae.

In the same passage the words *et collocauit me* come from I Kings II 24, *Dominus qui firmauit me et conlocauit super solium Dauid patris mei*, where *Salomon sapiens* is speaking. In 2e he quotes Psalm CXVIII 112, *inclinaui cor meum ad faciendas iustificationes tuas in aeternum propter retributionem*, and in the parallel passage 2'e he alludes to I Thessalonians III 9, *quam enim gratiarum actionem possumus Deo retribuere pro uobis*. A backward glance to 2e with its repeated quotation, *sicut et ceteris* from I Thessalonians V 6, brings attention to another feature of Patrick's ordering of his text, citation of the same Biblical sources in paired paragraphs.

In 1 he quotes Mark XIII 19, 'the Little Apocalypse', I Thessalonians V 6, Hebrews VII 19, John VIII 43-4, and Luke's Acts XXII 3, with which compare 1', where he quotes Apocalypse XIX 5, I Thessalonians II 10, III 13, V 23, Hebrews XII 28, John IV 10, and Luke's Gospel XXIV 19. In 2 he quotes Ecclesiastes I 8, I Thessalonians V 6, and Psalm CXVIII 112, with which compare 2', where he quotes Ecclesiastes IV 13, I Thessalonians III 9, and Psalm CXVIII 67.

At the centre of the entire passage in 3 Patrick presents the climax of his argument, which he crowns with long quotations from the Bible. The

words which frame the quotations are also Biblical. The formula *et si* . . .
sed, which he uses in the first two sentences, is from Paul, II Corinthians V
16; *scriptum est enim* is found in Matthew IV 6, *quanto magis* in Matthew VI
30, *et iterum* in Matthew XIX 24. The citations are carefully ordered. The
words *tardiori lingua* echo Exodus IV 10, the excuse offered by Moses to
God, *inpeditioris et tardioris linguae sum*. That does not matter to God, for as
Isaiah XXXII 4 says, 'Stammering tongues will swiftly learn to speak peace'.
The verses which follow immediately, which Patrick does not quote but
doubtless expects his audience to know, are:

> non uocabitur ultra is qui insipiens est princeps
> neque fraudulentus appellabitur maior.

Patrick increases the tension with *quanto magis* and then makes a very
bold alteration. At II Corinthians III 2 Paul wrote *epistula nostra uos estis*,
and at Acts XIII 47 Luke wrote *ut sis in salutem usque ad extremum terrae*,
quoting (with an economy suitable for Patrick, who has just quoted the
prophet) Isaiah XLIX 6, *ut sis salus mea usque ad extremum terrae*. Patrick
shows that he knows very well he has changed Paul's meaning by placing
qui sumus before *inquit*. Patrick's claim is now, '*I am* the letter of Christ',
but by using a third person verb, *inquit*, he attributes the claim to St Paul.
He repeats Paul's words *et si* . . . *sed* and returns to the quotation from II
Corinthians III 3, *scripta non atramento sed Spiritu Dei uiui*. For his final blast
Patrick affirms that the Holy Spirit Himself declares 'even rustic work
created by the Most High', citing Ecclesiasticus VII 16. Bieler suggests that
Patrick 'apparently mistakes *rusticatio* (γεωργία) for *rusticitas* (ἀγροικία)'.[22] One
should not assume that Patrick mistook anything. He has already said that
he, the letter of Christ, if not learned, is still valid and very vigorous. His
concern here is less with rustic style than with his life and work, hard work
in the country, his mission at the end of the earth in Ireland, where he,
primus rusticus, 'the extreme rustic', 'the most remote countryman', knows
most certainly what God in His mercy has done.

Every word of Patrick's Apology is in its correct place. The climax of
his argument is the quotation from Ecclesiasticus VII 16 in part 3, in the
central line of this eighty-five-lined passage, forty-three lines from the
beginning and forty-three lines from the end. The word *testatur*, which
introduces it,[23] is 245th from the beginning, and the word *unde*, which
follows it, is 245th from the end. There are 2724 letters, of which the
central fall exactly at the centre of *Et iterum Spiritus testatur*.

Each paragraph is also carefully ordered. In part 1 Patrick's obsession is
with language and letters: *scribere, linguam hominum, iura et sacras litteras,
sermones, sermo et loquela, linguam alienam, scripturae, in sermonibus, linguam,*

22 Bieler, *Libri* XII 123.
23 See below p. 106.

perlegeram, dixero, praefatus sum. There are twenty lines and 125 words. The central phrase is *ex saliua scripturae meae* at the end of the central tenth line, the word *scripturae* being sixty-third from the beginning and sixty-third from the end. There are exactly 700 letters, of which the 350th is the last of *ex saliua scripturae meae*. In part 2 Patrick is obsessed with style. There are fifty-five words. The central phrase is *quia disertis breuitate sermone explicare nequeo*, the word *breuitate* being twenty-eighth from the beginning and twenty-eighth from the end. In part 3 there are seventy words. The central phrase is *qui sumus inquit epistola Xpisti*, the centre falling between *inquit* and *epistola*. In part 2' Patrick tells what God has done despite his ignorance, *in sua misericordia sustulit me*. There are seventy-five words, of which *misericordia* is thirty-eighth from the beginning and thirty-eighth from the end. In part 1' there are 170 words. The central phrase is *ut cum humilitate et ueraciter deseruirem illis*, *et ueraciter* being the central words.

Note also in part 1' the sequence of 4-3-2-1-2-3-4 words in a, two parallel clauses of seven words each in b, and two parallel phrases of four words each in c. In 1'a there are twenty-two syllables from i to iii inclusive and twenty-three syllables from iv to i' inclusive, forty-nine letters from i to iii and fifty letters from iv to i'.

In part 1 the golden section of 125 falls at 77 and 48. The seventy-seventh word is *linguam* in the quotation from Ecclesiasticus IV 29. In part 3 the golden section of 70 falls at 43 and 27. The twenty-seventh word is *pacem*, the last of the quotation from Isaiah XXXII 4. In part 2' the golden section of 75 falls at 46 and 29. The twenty-ninth word is *profundo* at the end of 2'c. In part 1' the golden section of 170 falls at 105 and 65. The 105th word is *aeternam* at the end of the thematic crux 1'div.

Patrick disposed words at arithmetically fixed intervals. In part 1, concerned with speech and language, the word *sermo* occurs three times, of which the third is sixty-ninth, *in sermonibus* 11. From the beginning of the passage to that point the central, thirty-fifth, word is *sermones* 7. From *sermones* 7 to *sermonibus* 11 inclusive there are thirty-five words, of which the golden section falls at 22 and 13. From *sermo* 9 to *sermonibus* 11 there are twenty-two words. *Sermo* 9 is the forty-eighth word of the 125-word passage, of which the golden section falls at 77 and 48.

From the beginning of part 1 *linguam* 3 is the fifteenth word (5×3). After that *linguam* 9 is the fortieth word (5×8). From *linguam* 12 to *lingua* 34 inclusive there are 120 words (5×24). Between *lingua* 34 and *linguae* 36 there are five words.

From the crux in part 3 to the end Patrick names God twelve times. Before the first *Xpisti* 38 there are 216 words (3×72). Between the first and the second *Spiritu Dei* 41 there are twenty-one words (3×7). From the second to the third *Spiritus* 42 inclusive there are six words (3×2). From the third to the fourth *Altissimo* 43 inclusive there are six words (3×2). From the fourth to the fifth *Domino* 54 inclusive there are sixty-three words (3 × 21). After the fifth the sixth *Deum* 58 is the twenty-fourth word (3 × 8). After the sixth the seventh *Xpisti* 68 is the sixtieth word (3 × 20). From the seventh to the eighth *Trinitatis* 71 inclusive there are twenty-four words (3 × 8). After the eighth the ninth *Dei* 73 is the ninth word (3 × 3). Between the ninth and the tenth *Dei* 76 there are six words (3 × 2). From the tenth to the eleventh *Domino* 78 inclusive there are eighteen words (3 × 6). From the eleventh to the twelfth *Dominus* 80 there are fifteen words (3 × 5), after which there are thirty words (3 × 10) to the end of the Apology. From the beginning of the Apology to the first *Xpisti* inclusive there are 217 words, and from the twelfth *Dominus* inclusive to the end there are thirty-one words, together 248 words, exactly half the 495 words of the Apology.

In the Book of Armagh there are larger initials at 1a *Quapropter*, 1b *Timui*, 1c *ET*, 1d *Nam*, and two punctuation marks after *combiberunt* 1b. There are larger initials in the first three words of the first long Biblical quotation, *Sapiens Per Linguam* 1d and in *Sicut* at the beginning of the last clause of 2d, in 3 in *Cum* and *tardiori*, in *scriptum*, and in the second *et si*, but most important, in the first letter of three of the climactic Biblical quotations, and in the last important word of all four. The last clause of 2'd begins with larger initials in *Et*. In 1' there are larger initials in the first and last clauses of a, three of them in di*a*, two in iii*a*, and at the crux in iv. There are also two punctuation marks after *Deum* at the crux of 1'aiv. Whether to mark textual puzzles or the symmetrical centres of paragraphs I do not know, but there are *Z*-marks in the margin against lines containing *ex saliua scripturae meae, quia disertis breuitate sermone explicare nequeo, qui sumus inquit epistola Xpisti,* and *et rusticationem ab Altissimo creatam.*

Here in a single chapter we see Patrick appearing to protest his ignorance and inelegance as he produces clausulae and cursus rhythms. He balances rhythmical patterns and words and ideas and quotations from Biblical sources. By judicious and economical quotation of the Bible he appears to concede some praise to his critics while actually attacking them. He shows more than once in this short passage that he knows how to build toward a rhetorical climax. In one paragraph, at the very centre in 3, he consecutively applies to himself the words of Moses, Isaiah, St Paul, St Luke, and Jesus ben Sirach, arrogates to himself the authority of Lawgiver, Prophet, Apostle, and Evangelist, and simultaneously uses the unquoted context of his quotations to attack his critics. If the stupendous claims Patrick makes for himself in this Apology have gone largely unnoticed that is because modern readers have paid attention more to what is apparently said than to what is really meant. The proof of what is really meant lies partly in the utter consistency with which Patrick leaves the sting of his remarks in the unquoted contexts of what he cites.

Although the Apology has no chiastic pair it is tightly bound, as the end of part **I**, to the beginning of part **I**. Note the following words and phrases in chapter I: *rusticissimus* 1, *capturam dedi* 8, *in captiuitate* 11, *tot milia hominum* 12, *usque ad ultimum terrae* 18, *inter alienigenas* 19, *adolescentiae* 24, *antequam scirem et antequam saperem* 25-6. Compare them with the following words and phrases in the Apology, chapter VII: *rusticationem* 43 and *rusticus* 44, *capturam dedi* 22, *post captiuitatem* 82, *tot milia hominum* 78, *usque ad ultimum terrae* 38, *in linguam alienam* 9, *adolescens* 21, *antequam scirem quid adpetere* 23.

Part **II** is a single chapter VIII (16-25) of eight paragraphs, seven chiastically arranged with an eighth appended to the seventh, in which Patrick defends the authenticity and integrity of his vocation. At the beginning in paragraph 1 (16-8) he relates chiastically his arrival in Ireland and his first vision, of return to Britain. Compare a *Dei* 4 with a' *Dei* 46; b *timor* 4 with b' *timorem* 46; c *fides* 5 with c' *fide* 43; di *audiui* 15 with d'i *audiissem* 34; dii *iturus* 16 with d'ii *ire* 33; diii *et iterum post paululum tempus* 17 with d'iii *et antequam orationem consummarem* 37; div *audiui responsum dicentem mihi* 18 with d'iv *audiui unum ex illis et fortiter exclamabat post me* 38-9; e *ecce nauis tua parata est* 19 with e' *perueni ad nauem illam* 28; the cause for fear in f *et non erat prope* 20 with his lack of fear in f' *et nihil metuebam* 28; his flight in g *et deinde postmodum conuersus sum in fugam* 24 with his route in g' *qui uiam meam ad bonum dirigebat* 27; around the crux relating his escape in h *et intermisi hominem cum quo fueram sex annis* 25 and the source of power which enabled his escape in h' *et ueni in uirtute Dei* 26. The passage contains fifty lines and 295 words. The central lines of the chiasmus are 25 and 26, and the central 148th word is *et* at the beginning of line 26. The golden section of the 295 words falls at 182 and 113. The passage ends *et protinus nauigauimus* 50. The 113th word from the end begins *unde nauigare cum illis* 30.

The pair to paragraph 1 is paragraph 1' (23-5), relating Patrick's arrival in Britain and two visions, of return to Ireland and of the Holy Spirit praying within him. Compare ai *rogauerunt me* 113 with a'i *rogamus te* 126, aii *ut* 114 with a'ii *ut* 127, aiii *nusquam ab illis discederem* 115 with a'iii *uenias et adhuc ambulas inter nos* 127, aiv *et legi* 120 with a'iv *et amplius non potui legere* 129, bi *principium epistolae* 120 with b'i *principium epistolae* 121, around the crux c *uox Hiberionacum* 120. At the end compare a"i *et sic expertus sum* 130 with a"'i *et sic expertus sum* 149, a"ii *uerbis peritissimis quos ego audiui et non potui intellegere* 136-7 with a"'ii *quae uerbis exprimi non possunt* 154, b" *nisi ad postremum orationis sic effitiatus est* 138 with b"' *sed ad postremum orationis sic effitiatus est* 148, c" *qui dedit animam suam pro te ipse est qui loquitur in te* 139-40 with c"' *quis esset qui in me orabat* 147, around the crux in d" 142-6.

To connect the beginning of part **II** with the end compare in paragraph 1 part 1, Patrick's arrival in Ireland, *sed postquam Hiberione deueneram* 1 with paragraph 1' part 1, his return to Britain, *et iterum post paucos annos in Brittanniis eram* 110, his career as a slave, 2 *cotidie itaque pecora pascebam* 2, with his reception as a returned son, 2 *cum parentibus meis qui me ut filium susceperunt* 111-2, his vision in Ireland telling him of return to Britain, 3 *et ibi scilicet quadam nocte in somno audiui uocem dicentem mihi "Bene ieiunas cito iturus ad patriam tuam"* 14-6, with his vision in Britain asking him to return to Ireland, 3 *et ibi scilicet uidi in uisu noctis uirum uenientem quasi de Hiberione* ... 116. These are the only two places in the *Confessio* in which Patrick uses the phrase *et ibi scilicet*. Compare also Patrick's account of God's answer even before completion of a prayer, 4 *et antequam orationem consummarem* 37 with his two accounts of illumination at the conclusion of prayer, 4 *nisi ad postremum orationis sic effitiatus est* 138, *sed ad postremum orationis sic effitiatus est* 148, the only occurrences of this phrase in the *Confessio*.

Paragraph 2 exhibits internal chiastic structure. Compare ai *et cibus defuit illis* 53 with a'i *ut hodie cibum mittat uobis* 64, aii *et fames inualuit super eos* 54 with a'ii *quia ubique abundabat illi* 65, bi *tu* 57 with b'i *ego* 61, bii *dicis* 57 with b'ii *dixi* 61, biii *Deus tuus* 57 with b'iii *Deum meum* 62, biv *magnus et omnipotens est* 57 with b'iv *quia nihil est impossibile illi* 63, around the crux in c *quia nos a fame periclitamur* 59. The paragraph is tightly composed of fifteen lines, which divide by extreme and mean ratio at 9 and 6. The crux of the chiasmus is the ninth line. There are ninety-five words, of which the central, forty-eighth, word is the first of the crux of the chiasmus.

To connect paragraph 2 with paragraph 2' compare 1 *et uiginti octo dies per desertum iter fecimus* 52 with 1 *sicut superius insinuaui uiginti et octo dies per desertum iter fecimus* 107-8, 2 *difficile est enim ut aliquem hominem umquam uideamus* 60 with 2 *et ea nocte qua peruenimus homines* 109, 3 *et cibus defuit illis* 53 and *ut hodie cibum mittat uobis* 64 with 3 *de cibo uero nihil habuimus* 109. These are the only places in the *Confessio* in which Patrick uses the phrase about the twenty-eight-day trek.

Paragraph 3 also exhibits internal chiastic structure. Compare a *adiuuante Deo* 66 with a' *Deo gratias* 79, bi *grex porcorum in uia ante oculos nostros apparuit* 67 with b'i *mel siluestre inuenerunt* 76, bii *et multos ex illis interfecerunt* 68 with b'ii *et mihi partem obtulerunt* 77, c *et ibi duas noctes manserunt et bene refecti* 69 with c' *et ex hac die cibum abundanter habuerunt* 75, around the crux in d *et post hoc summas gratias egerunt Deo* 73 and d' *et ego honorificatus sum sub oculis eorum* 74. The paragraph is tightly composed of fifteen lines, which divide by symmetry at the eighth line and by extreme and mean ratio at 9 and 6. The central eighth line is the beginning of the crux of the chiasmus, and the ninth line is the end of the crux of the chiasmus. The eighty-five words divide by symmetry at 43 and by extreme and mean ratio at 53 and 32. The golden section of words falls in the golden section line 9 at *et ego | honorificatus sum*. Note the phrases *summas gratias egerunt Deo* 73 and *Deo gratias* 79. Between *gratias* 73 and *gratias* 79 there are thirty-two words. Note the phrases *ante oculos nostros* 67 and *sub oculis eorum* 74. Between *oculos* 67 and *oculis* 74 there are forty-three words. Note the phrases *adiuuante Deo* 66, *gratias egerunt Deo* 73, and *Deo gratias* 79. From *Deo* 66 to *Deo* 79 inclusive there are seventy-nine words, which divide by extreme and mean ratio at 49 and 30. From *Deo* 66 to *Deo* 73 inclusive there are forty-nine words. Note also *uiam* 64, *uia* 67, and *uiam* 72. From *uiam* 64 to *uiam* 72 inclusive there are fifty words, which divide by extreme and mean ratio at 31 and 19. *Uia* 67 is the nineteenth word after *uiam* 64. From *uia* 64 to *uiam* 72 inclusive there are thirty-one words.

Paragraph 3' also exhibits internal chiasmus. Compare a *ea nocte prima* 98 with a' *decimo die* 106, b *duobus mensibus* 100 with b' *nocte illa sexagesima* 102, around the crux in c *quod ita factum est* 101.

To connect paragraph 3 with paragraph 3' compare 1 *ita factum est* 66 with 1 *ita factum est* 101, 2 *duas noctes manserunt* 69 with 2 *ea nocte prima itaque mansi cum illis* 98 and *duobus mensibus eris cum illis* 100, 3 *cibum abundanter habuerunt* 75 with 3 *praeuidit nobis cibum* 104. These are the only two places in which Patrick uses the phrase *ita factum est*, in the first line of paragraph 3 and a central line of paragraph 3'.

The crucial paragraph 4 of the chiastically ordered part **II** exhibits internal chiasmus. Compare a *eadem uero nocte* 81 with a' *in illa die* 94, b *et fortiter temptauit me Satanas* 82 with b' *et credo quod a Xpisto Domino meo subuentus sum et Spiritus eius iam tunc clamabat pro me* 91-2, c *et cecidit super me ueluti saxum ingens et nihil membrorum meorum praeualens* 84-5 with c' *et statim discussit a me omnem grauitudinem* 90, di *ut Heliam uocarem* 86 with d'i *dum clamarem "Helia, Helia"* 88, dii *uidi in caelum solem oriri* 87 with d'ii *splendor solis illius decidit super me* 89. The 155 lines of part **II** divide by extreme and mean ratio at 96 and 59. The last of the crucial paragraph 4 is line 96.

Patrick introduces this story by describing it as his temptation in the dark: *eadem uero nocte eram dormiens et fortiter temptauit me Satanas*. His diction recalls the dark moment of the temptation of Jesus in Matthew XXVII 45-51:

> tenebrae factae sunt super uniuersam terram … "Heli, Heli" … hoc est "Deus meus, Deus meus" … "Uideamus an ueniat Helias liberans eum" … et petrae scissae sunt.

It also involves word play on Ηλιας 'Elijah', Ηλι 'my God', and ἥλιος 'sun'.

Note Patrick's disposition of the words *orare*, *Spiritus*, and *oratio* : *orabam* 3, *Spiritus* 5, *orationes* 6, *orationem* 9, *Spiritus* 13, *orare* 36, making a pattern A-B-C-C-B-A. Then more complex: *orationem* 37, *orare* 58, *Spiritus* 92, *Spiritus* 96, *orationis* 138, *orantem* 142, *orabat* 145, *orabat* 147, *orationis* 148, *Spiritus* 148, *Spiritus* 151, *orationis* 151, *oremus* 152, *Spiritus* 153, making a pattern C-A-B-B-C-A-A-A-C-B-B-C-A-B. The Spirit is named seven times, three times before and and three times after the climactic last line of the central paragraph. The noun *oratio* occurs three times before and three times after the central paragraph.

The 155 lines of part **II** divide by extreme and mean ratio at 96 and 59, and the 937 words divide by extreme and mean ratio at 579 and 358. The ninety-sixth line is the last of the central chapter. The 579th word, *testatur*, introduces the final quotation of the central chapter, *non uos estis qui loquimini sed Spiritus Patris uestri qui loquitur in uobis*. The same verb, *testatur*, introduces the central quotation of the Apology in chapter VII.[24]

The pair to the chiastically arranged part **II**, authenticating Patrick's vocation, is the chiastically arranged part **IIII**, authenticating his mission. Compare 1 the first line, *et ibi opto 'impendere' eam* [*sc. animam meam*] *'usque ad mortem'*, with 1' the last line 218, *ut meipsum 'impendar pro animabus uestris'*, both with echoes of II Corinthians XII 15. Compare 2 the second line, *si Dominus mihi indulgeret*, with 2' the penultimate line 217, *potens est Dominus ut det mihi postmodum*. Compare what God has given to Patrick in 3, lines 3-4, *quia ualde 'debitor sum' Deo qui mihi tantam gratiam donauit*, with its echo of Romans I 14, with what Patrick has given in 3', lines 196-213, *interim praemia dabam regibus, quantum ego erogaui illis, pretium quindecim hominum distribui illis, ita ut me 'fruamini', et ego 'uobis' semper 'fruar' in Deum*, with its echo of Romans XV 24.

Many readers have puzzled over Patrick's assertion that he paid money to kings and the sons of kings and the brehons, *qui iudicabant per omnes regiones* 209. Why should he have distributed the price of fifteen men to those who judged in Ireland? One answer may be that he knew the Biblical Book of Judges, in which fifteen men are said to have judged in Israel.

Part 4 exhibits internal chiasmus. Compare a *populi* 5 with a' *populum* 30, b *renascerentur* 5 with b' *baptizarent* 29, c *clerici* 7 with c'*clerici* 29, di *uenientem ad credulitatem* 8 with d'i *uenturi sunt credentes* 21, dii *Dominus* 9 with d'ii *Dominus* 23, diii *promiserat per prophetas* 10 with d'iii *dicit per prophetas* 25, div 11-13 the quotation from Jeremiah XVI 19 with d'iv 26 the quotation from Jeremiah XVI 16, around the crux in e *et ibi uolo expectare promissum ipsius* 16.

To connect part 4 with part 4' compare 1 *ut populi multi per me in Deum renascerentur et postmodum consummarentur* 5-6 and *qui baptizarent* 29 with 1 *forte autem quando baptizaui tot milia hominum* 178 and *populum consummaret* 192, 2 *et ut clerici ubique illis ordinarentur* 7 with 2 *aut quando ordinauit ubique Dominus clericos* 181 and *aut clericos ordinaret* 191, 3 *ad extremum terrae* 15 with 3 *ad exteras partes* 187.

To connect part 5 with part 5' compare *monachi et uirgines Xpisti* 63 with *fratribus Xpistianis et uirginibus Xpisti* 167-8.

Part 6 exhibits internal chiasmus. Compare a *Domini* 91 with a' *Dominus* 101, bi *ego* 92 with b'i *ego* 97, bii *sed alligatus Spiritu* 93 with b'ii *sed Xpistus Dominus* 98, biii *qui mihi protestatur* 94 with b'iii *qui me imperauit* 99, biv *ut*

24 See above pp. 58, 100.

futurum reum me esse designat 95 with b'iv *ut uenirem esse cum illis residuum aetatis meae* 100, around the crux in c *et timeo perdere laborem quem inchoaui* 96. The nineteen lines divide by extreme and mean ratio at 12 and 7, and the ninety-six words divide by extreme and mean ratio at 59 and 37. The fifty-ninth word is the first of line 12, the crux of the chiasmus.

Part 6' also exhibits internal chiasmus. Compare a *unde autem debueram* 125 with a' *quod ante debueram* 146, b *gratias* 125 with b' *gratiam* 145, c *insipientiae meae neglegentiae meae* 126-7 with c' *rusticitatem meam* 144, around the crux in d *quia uidit in me quod paratus eram* 134 and d' *sed quod mihi pro his nesciebam* 135. The twenty-two lines divide by symmetry at 11 and 11. The 130 words divide by symmetry at 65 and 65. The sixty-fifth word occurs at the end of the eleventh line at the crux of the chiasmus d'.

To connect part 6 with part 6' compare 1 *unde autem* 85 with 1 *unde autem* 125, 2 *paratus eram* 87 with 2 *paratus eram* 134, both quotations from Psalm CXVIII 60, 3 *sed alligatus Spiritu* 93 with 3 *et sicut Spiritus suggerebat* 132.

The crux of the chiasmus of part **IIII**, part 7, beginning *spero autem hoc debueram* 104, echoes the beginning of the preceding part 6, *unde autem etsi uoluero* 85, and is echoed by the beginning of part 6', *unde autem debueram* 125. It exhibits internal chiasmus. Compare a *quia fortis est qui cotidie nititur subuertere me a fide* 107 with a' *et usque nunc fauente Domino fidem seruaui* 119, b *et praeposita castitate religionis non fictae* 108 with b' *creuit in me amor Dei et timor ipsius* 118, c *usque in finem uitae meae* 109 with c' *a iuuentute mea* 117, d *Domino meo* 109 with d' *Domino meo* 114, e *sed caro inimica semper trahit ad mortem* 110 with e' *uitam perfectam ego non egi* 112, around the crux in f *id est ad inlecebras inlicitate perficiendas* 111. The twenty-one lines divide by extreme and mean ratio at 13 and 8, and the 134 words divide by extreme and mean ratio at 83 and 51, at the last two words of the eighth line 111, at the crux of the chiasmus f.

The 1305 words of part **IIII** divide by extreme and mean ratio at 807 and 498, in the phrase *in milia | milium* XX 133.

The central part **III** of the *Confessio* comprises eleven chapters VIIII-XVIIII (26-36), which relate Patrick's dealings with his ecclesiastical superiors and antagonists.

The first chapter VIIII H exhibits internal chiasmus. Compare a *temptatus sum* 1 with a' *humiliatus sum* 22, b *impulsus sum* 3 with b' *castigatus sum* 21, c *Deum* 9 with c' *Deum* 18, d *occasionem post annos triginta inuenerunt me aduersus* 10 with d' *habebam tunc annos quindecim* 17, e *uerbum quod confessus fueram antequam essem diaconus* 11 with e' *quae in pueritia mea una die gesseram* 13, around the crux in f *propter anxietatem maesto animo insinuaui amicissimo meo* 12. The twenty-three lines divide by symmetry at 12, and the 138 words divide by extreme and mean ratio at 85 and 53. The fifty-third word from the beginning is *obprobrium* 8. The eighty-fifth word from the beginning is the last of line 12, the end of the crux of the chiasmus, *amicissimo meo*.

To connect the first chapter VIIII H with the last XVIIII H' compare 1 *aliquantis senioribus meis* 1 with 1 *aliquantos de senioribus meis* 3, 2 *peregrino* 5 with 2 *peregrinationis* 9, 3 *propter nomen suum* 6 with *pro nomine eius* 14, 4 *obprobrium* 8 with *obprobrium* 9, 5 *animo* 12 with *animam* 13, 6 *in incredulitate* 20 with *ab incredulis* 8. These are the only two places in the *Confessio* in which Patrick uses the words *obprobrium, peregrinus, peregrinatio,* and the phrase *seniores mei.* The twenty-three lines of H and the fourteen lines of H' comprise thirty-seven lines, which divide by extreme and mean ratio at 23 and 14.

To connect the second chapter X J with the penultimate XVIII J' compare 1 *donec deficiebam* 2, a quotation from Psalm XVII 38, with 1 *numerum dierum noueram* 3, a quotation from Psalm XXXVIII 5, 2 *et aptauit me ut hodie essem quod aliquando longe a me erat* 5-6 with 2 *unde mihi haec sapientia quae in me non erat* 1-2, 3 *ut ego curam haberem aut satagerem pro salute aliorum* 7-8 with 3 *unde mihi postmodum donum tam magnum tam salubre* 5.

To connect the third chapter XI K with the antepenultimate XVII K' compare 1 *responsum diuinum* 5 with 1 *responsum diuinum* 10, both quotations from Romans XI 4, and 2 *qui uos tangit quasi qui tangit pupillam oculi mei* 10-1 with 2 *ut me pauperculum pupillum idiotam* 9-10. Both chapters contain sixty-two words. In the former the quotation containing the word *pupillam* begins at the fifty-fourth word. In the latter the clause containing the word *pupillum* begins at the fifty-fourth word. In the former the phrase *responsum diuinum* begins at the thirtieth word. In the latter the phrase *responsum diuinum* ends at the sixtieth word.

Chapter XVI L' exhibits internal chiasmus and parallelism:

1		a	unde ergo indefessam gratiam ago Deo meo
2	4	b	qui me fidelem seruauit in die temptationis meae
3		c	ita ut hodie confidenter offeram illi sacrificium
3		c'	ut hostiam uiuentem animam meam Xpisto Domino meo
2		b'	qui me seruauit ab omnibus angustiis meis
1		a'	aequaliter debeo suscipere et Deo gratias semper agere
2		b"	qui mihi ostendit
3		c"	hoc opus tam pium et tam mirificum.

To connect chapter XVI L' with chapter XII L compare the parts numbered 1 above with 1 *idcirco gratias ago ei* 1, 2 with 2 *qui me in omnibus confortauit* 2, 3 with 3 *et de mea quoque opera quod a Xpisto Domino meo didiceram* 4, and 4 above *fidelem* with 4 *et fides mea probata est* 6.

To connect chapter XIII M with chapter XV M' compare 1 *unde autem audenter dico* 1 with *satis dico … audenter rursus* 1 and 10, 2 *'teste Deo' habeo* 4 with 2 *sed scit Deus* 11, 3 *'quia non sum mentitus' in sermonibus quos ego retuli uobis* 5-6 with 3 *forsitan tacuissem propter 'caritatem Xpisti'* 12. The former chapter echoes II Corinthians I 23 and the latter II Corinthians V 4. Only in these two chapters does Patrick use the phrase *audenter dico.*

The crux of the chiasmus of part **III** is chapter XIIII N, which exhibits internal chiasmus. Compare a *me* 8 with a' *me* 15, b *ille* 9 with b' *illi* 13, c *in mea absentia pulsaret pro me* 9 with c' *quod non eram dignus* 12, around the crux in d *etiam mihi ipse ore suo dixerat* 10 and d' *ecce dandus es tu ad gradum episcopatus* 11. In the first line of this chapter Patrick grieves for his friend, *sed magis doleo pro amicissimo meo*. This was the man who *etiam mihi ipse ore suo dixerat "Ecce dandus es tu ad gradum episcopatus"*. The seventeen lines of this chapter divide by extreme and mean ratio at 11 and 6. The ninety words of this chapter divide by extreme and mean ratio at 56 and 34. The eleventh line is *Ecce dandus es* | *tu* | *ad gradum episcopatus*, and the fifty-sixth word is the central word of that line, *tu*. From the beginning of part **III** to the beginning of this central chapter exclusive there are fifty-five lines, and from the beginning of this central chapter to the end of part **III** inclusive there are eighty-nine lines, together 144, which divide by extreme and mean ratio at 89 and 55. From the beginning of part **III** to the end of this central chapter inclusive there are seventy-two lines, and thence to the end of part **III** there are also seventy-two lines.

The noun *episcopatus* VIIII 2 and XIIII 11 connects the beginning of part **III** with golden section line of the central chapter of part **III**. So does the phrase *amicissimo meo*, which connects the first line of the first chapter of part **III** VIIII 12 and the golden section line of the central chapter of part **III** XIIII 11. The phrases *ab aliquantis senioribus meis* VIIII 1, *ab aliquantis fratribus* XIIII 4, and *aliquantos de senioribus meis* XVIIII 3 link the beginning of part **III** with the crux and the end.

Chapter XIIII is the centre not only of part **III** but of the entire *Confessio*, which comprises in the present analysis twenty-six chapters and 4570 words. The central 2285th word of the entire text is *Ecce dandus es* | *tu* | *ad gradum episcopatus*.

Patrick took further care to bind together the five parts of the *Confessio*. The phrase *capturam dedi* links the beginning and the end of part **I**, chapter I line 8 and chapter VII line 22, to the crux of part **II** chapter VIII line 97. The proper noun *Hiberione* links the beginning of part **I**, chapter I line 11, to the beginning of part **II**, chapter VIII line 1, as well as to the end of part **V**, chapter XXVI line 5. The noun *diaconus* links the beginning of part **I**, chapter I line 4, to the beginning of part **III**, chapter VIIII line 11, as do the phrases *annorum tunc fere sedecim* I 9 and *habebam tunc annos quindecim* VIIII 17. The nouns *presbyter* I 5 and *senior* VIIII 1 and XVIIII 3 link the beginning of part **I** with the beginning and the end of part **III**. So do the nouns *incredulitas* I 20, VIIII 20, and *incredulus* XVIIII 8. The words *humilitatem* I 23, *humiliarer* VII 47, *cum humilitate* VII 70, and *humiliatus sum* VIIII 22 link the beginning and the end of part **I** with the beginning of part **III**. The phrases *et … temptauit me Satanas* VIII 82 and *et … temptatus sum ab aliquantis senioribus* VIIII 1 link the crux of part **II** to the beginning of part **III**. The word *pusillus* VII 58 and XXVI 7 and the phrases *post obitum meum*

VII 77 and *antequam moriar* XXVI 12 link the end of part **I** with the end of part **V**. The phrase *quia non mentior* XX 116 and XXI 2 links the crux of part **IIII** with the beginning of part **V**, and the phrase *usque in finem uitae meae* XX 109 links the central line of part **IIII** with XXVI 12, the end of part **V**.

The Biblical models for this fivefold division of the *Confessio*[25] are the five books of the Pentateuch and their New Testament reflex in the five collections of sayings of Jesus in St Matthew's Gospel.

Part **I** corresponds to Genesis, relating Patrick's beginnings and early history, rising to the first great climax in the Apology, where the concern with language may be compared with the account of Babel and Patrick's captivity in Ireland may be compared with Joseph's captivity in Egypt.

Part **II** corresponds to Exodus, in which the herdsman Patrick escapes from captivity across the sea like the shepherd Moses. His journey of four weeks through the desert may be compared with the Israelites' journey of four decades through the desert, his miraculous feeding with their manna, the provision of fire during his journey with the pillar of fire during the Israelites' journey, his vision of God with Moses's vision of God on Mount Sinai.

Part **III** corresponds to Leviticus, relating Patrick's dealings with ecclesiastical authorities and his own ecclesiastical status.

Part **IIII** corresponds to Numbers, relating Patrick's account of his conversions, baptisms, confirmations, and ordinations, *plus augetur numerus ... nescimus numerum eorum* 77-9.

Part **V** corresponds to Deuteronomy, concluding with Patrick's preparation for death.

In chapter XVII Patrick writes *de periculis duodecim qua periclitata est anima mea*, which most readers have assumed to be unspecified. Patrick may, however, have referred to all of them. The first was the earliest, whatever things he confessed *maesto animo insinuaui amicissimo meo quae in pueritia mea una die gesseram* **III** VIIII 12-3 (27). Second was the kidnap and enslavement related in **I** I (1-2), which followed a year after the sin. Third was the danger of his escape to a place two hundred miles distant, where he had never been and where he knew no one, but during which *nihil metuebam* **II** VIII 21-8 (17). Fourth was the perilous involvement with his fellow travellers, who first refused him passage, then asked him to join in a pagan ceremony of promising fidelity by sucking their nipples **II** VIII 29-50 (18). Fifth with the same men he nearly starved, then almost ate forest honey which had been offered in pagan sacrifice **II** VIII 51-80 (19). Sixth was the night on which *fortiter temptauit me Satanas* **II** VIII 81-96 (20). Seventh was another captivity of sixty days' duration many years later **II** VIII 97-103 (21). Eighth was at the crux of the account of the mission to Ireland, another temptation by Satan

25 I owe thanks to Sister Máire Bríd de Paor for suggesting that the *Confessio* is
    'like a five-act drama'.

quia fortis est qui cotidie nititur subuertere me a fide **IIII** XX 107 (44). Ninth was the objection of critics who asked *Iste quare se mittit in periculo inter hostes qui Deum non nouerunt?* **IIII** XX 139-40 (46). Tenth was the imprisonment of fourteen days' duration and confiscation of goods **IIII** XX 199-206 (52). Eleventh was the murder and enslavement of Patrick's catechumens related in the *Epistola*, when *praeualuit iniquitas iniquorum super nos* **III** 161 (16). That provoked Patrick's excommunication of Coroticus, which may have led in turn to the ecclesiastical trial of Patrick by British ecclesiastical *seniores*. The revelation of the first of Patrick's perils, the sin committed in boyhood, was the occasion for the twelfth, when Patrick saw *in uisu noctis quod scriptum erat contra faciem meam sine honore* **III** XI 3-4 (29).

Note the arrangement of these perils. The first is closely connected to the twelfth, the first related in the first chapter of part **III** VIIII (26), and the twelfth in the third chapter of part **III** XI (29) K, the chiastic pair to chapter XVII (35) K' in which he writes *de periculis duodecim*. The second, which is related first, is God's corrective punishment for the sin committed in boyhood in Britain, kidnap and enslavement in Ireland, and the eleventh is the kidnap and enslavement of Patrick's converts in Britain, which brings him into conflict with British ecclesiastical authorities and leads to the trial and dispute about episcopal status which is the crux of the *Confessio*. The third, fourth, and fifth involve pagans during Patrick's escape from Ireland. The ninth and tenth also involve pagans in Ireland. The sixth and eighth are temptations by Satan. The seventh is the sixty days' captivity.

Closely bound with Patrick's account of the twelve perils from which God rescued him is his account of seven visions in which God revealed to him His purpose and Himself.

The first vision he records at the beginning of part **II**, where he makes patterns of the words *orare*, *Spiritus*, and *oratio*.[26] There at VIII 14-9 (17) he writes

> et ibi scilicet quadam nocte in somno
> audiui uocem dicentem mihi
> "Bene ieiunas cito iturus ad patriam tuam"
> et iterum post paululum tempus
> audiui responsum dicentem mihi
> "Ecce nauis tua parata est".

First a voice tells Patrick that he is to return home; then an answer tells him how he is to return. The voice speaks seven words and the answer five, together twelve, which divide by extreme and mean ratio at 7 and 5.

The second vision Patrick records at the crux of part **II** VIII 81-96 (20). Again he was sleeping:

26 See above pp. 105-6.

> Eadem uero nocte eram dormiens
> et fortiter temptauit me Satanas,

who paralysed him. Patrick asks

> unde me uenit ignaro in spiritu ut Heliam uocarem?

The last word of the question is the fortieth of the chapter. The fortieth word after that answers the question:

> Spiritus eius iam tunc clamabat pro me.

That chapter, at the crux of part **II**, ends

> Dominus testatur "Non uos estis qui loquimini
> sed Spiritus Patris uestri qui loquitur in uobis.

The third vision Patrick relates directly after this VIII 97-103 (21). Again he heard 'an answer' at night:

> Et iterum post annos multos adhuc capturam dedi.
> Ea nocte prima itaque mansi cum illis
> responsum autem diuinum audiui dicentem mihi
> "Duobus mensibus eris cum illis"
> quod ita factum est.
> Nocte illa sexagesima
> liberauit me Dominus de manibus eorum.

In the fourth vision, VIII 110-33 (23), a man named in a dream presented innumerable letters. As Patrick recited the beginning of one of them he imagined himself 'hearing at that very moment the voice of those very men who were beside the Forest of Foclut'. Now, thanks to God, their request has been fulfilled

> quia post plurimos annos praestitit illis Dominus
> secundum clamorem illorum.

In the account of the fifth vision, related in the very next lines, VIII 134-41 (24),

> Et alia nocte nescio, Deus scit,
> utrum in me an iuxta me,
> uerbis peritissimis quos ego audiui
> et non potui intellegere
> nisi ad postremum orationis sic effitiatus est

"Qui dedit animam suam pro te
ipse est qui loquitur in te"
et sic expergefactus sum gaudibundus.

In the account of the sixth vision, related in the very next lines, VIII 142–55 (25),

Et iterum uidi in me ipsum orantem
et eram quasi intra corpus meum
et audiui super me, hoc est super interiorem hominem,
et ibi fortiter orabat gemitibus
et inter haec stupebam et admirabam et cogitabam
quis esset qui in me orabat
sed ad postremum orationis sic effitiatus est ut sit Spiritus ... .

Patrick states in explicit and vivid detail that he both saw and heard someone praying inside his own body, who at the end of the prayer identified Himself as the Holy Spirit.

In the account of the seventh vision, related in part **III** XI (29), the chiastic pair to the chapter which mentions the twelve perils, Patrick writes

Igitur in illo die quo reprobatus sum
a memoratis supradictis
ad noctem illam uidi in uisu noctis
quod scriptum erat contra faciem meam sine honore
et inter haec audiui responsum diuinum dicentem mihi
"Male uidimus faciem designati nudato nomine"
nec sic praedixit "Male uidisti"
sed "Male uidimus"
quasi sibi me iunxisset
sicut dixit "Qui uos tangit
quasi qui tangit pupillam oculi mei".

Patrick states that six of the visions, all but the sixth, occurred at night, five of them explicitly, all of them presumably, in dreams of the utmost clarity and vividness. Note the progressive expansion of his perception. In the first vision Patrick simply heard a voice and an answer speaking to him, not explicitly divine, but reassuring, and credible because proven in fulfilment. The second vision was terrifying. Patrick was paralysed and impotent until from without, 'whence came to me in my ignorant spirit that I should call Elias'. Only later does he state that this came from the Spirit. In the third vision Patrick heard 'an answer', which was proven like the former in fulfilment, but specified here as 'divine'. In the fourth vision, after receiving from a man 'coming as if from Ireland' a letter 'containing "the

Voice of the Irish"' Patrick imagined hearing the very voice of the Irish. With the words of the dream proven again in fulfilment, *et sic expertus sum* 'and thus I have learned by experience', Patrick attributes the fulfilment to the Lord, 'after very many years the Lord has supplied them according to their clamour'. In the fifth vision Patrick is taken beyond what he knows, 'I do not know, God knows', in uncertain circumstances, 'whether within me or beside me', in which

> in most learned words I heard those whom
> I could not yet understand,
> except that at the very end of the prayer one spoke out thus:
> "He Who has given His own soul for you
> He it is Who speaks in you",
> and thus I was awakened rejoicing.

This fifth vision, which takes him beyond what he knows and in which Christ speaks in him, is the first to have induced joy. The account of the sixth vision is astounding. Not in the order he tells us, but from the inside out, Patrick sees his own 'interior man', above whom someone else is praying, whom Patrick both hears and sees, as if inside his own body, without leaving his own body. The Someone is the Spirit. The layers of seeing and relating are wonderfully presented, Patrick seeing within himself the Spirit who is overseeing his interior man, the Spirit both praying over the interior man and informing Patrick Who He is, so that he may relate this to us without. The account of the seventh vision crowns all the others. Patrick hears

> the divine answer saying to me
> "We have seen badly [*i.e.* 'with disapproval'] the face of the man
> marked out with his name stripped naked",
> and He did not say forth, "You have seen badly",
> but "We have seen badly",
> as if He had joined me to Himself,
> just as He has said, "He who touches you
> [is] as he who touches the pupil of my eye".

Having seen God praying within his own body Patrick now writes as if God had joined him to Himself as closely as to the pupil of an eye. In the chapter which immediately follows **III** XII (30) Patrick at the beginning thanks God *qui me in omnibus confortauit* 'Who has strengthened me in all things' and at the end affirms that *fides mea probata est coram Deo et hominibus* 'my faith was approved before God and men'. Later at **III** XVI 8 (34) he addresses God *qui mihi tanta diuinitate comparuisti* 'Who have appeared to me with such divinity'.

Patrick states in the account of his second vision that the Holy Spirit speaks through him, in the account of the fifth that Christ, 'He Who has given His own soul for you, He it is Who speaks in you', in the account of the sixth that he has actually heard the Holy Spirit praying inside his own body, and in the seventh that he has been joined to the Trinity as closely as to 'the pupil of my eye'.

These are large claims. Those who have believed Patrick supposing him to be simple and artless and clumsy need not disbelieve him knowing that he was not. These narratives may have been wrought after years of meditation on their meaning, but that does not falsify the ring of truth in each of them and in the entire sequence. They are the testament of a man trying to apprehend the Providence of God in his turbulent life, and they bear comparison with other great attempts by Augustine of Hippo, Boethius, and Abaelard.

Patrick's prose is rhythmical. In the entire *Confessio*, of lines containing more than four syllables and not ending entirely in Biblical quotation, only three, lines VIII 43, XX 200, and XXIIII 10, do not exhibit one of the commonly accepted cursus rhythms. All of them would conform to acceptable rhythms after reversing the order of the last words.

This is by no means an exhaustive analysis of the *Epistola* and the *Confessio*. But it should suffice to suggest that the modern scholars' picture of Patrick — a naive and barely literate rustic struggling to express himself in a language he could not master — is a grotesque misrepresentation of the thought and prose of a writer who was more than competent. That view of a simple, transparent, inarticulate, artless writer, which has issued from a fundamental inability to read and hear the words of a great saint, may now be consigned to the dustbin of our intellectual history, as we begin to learn, fifteen centuries after his death, to listen to him.

INFERENCES

Now we may address some of the questions over which so much scholarly ink has been spilled and so much acrimony generated. First, the problem of dates. Patrick states that he came from a family with enough social status to claim nobility and enough wealth to own land and slaves of both sexes. The men of his family were imperial officials both secular and ecclesiastical, yet only nominally Christian: his grandfather Potitus was a *presbyter*, and his father Calpornius was a *diaconus* and a *decurio*, a member of a civilian council responsible for collection of taxes.[27] As deficiencies in the revenue raised had to be made good from the private property of *decuriones* some entered holy orders in an attempt to defend themselves from confiscation. But that course should have entailed the surrender of property to their next of kin. Maintenance of status as both *decurio* and *diaconus* and retention of a *uillula* may imply that Calpornius had entered holy orders as a means of tax-avoidance, if not of tax-evasion, a possibility consistent with Patrick's statement that the religion of his childhood was not fervent. He refers to his fatherland as *Brittanniae* 'the Britains' and the neighbouring regions as *Galliae* 'the Gauls', implying a period in which Britain and Gaul were both divided into several provinces of the Roman Empire. As the civilian administration of Roman Britain was still functioning during Patrick's infancy and boyhood one infers that he was born before A.D. 410. He addresses the *Epistola ad Milites Corotici* to those serving a man whose name survives in modern Cardigan, Old Welsh *Ceredigion*, a man exercising *tyrannidem* as a petty king, a successor to imperial power in post-Roman Britain, after 410. As Patrick contrasts the practice of Coroticus with that of Roman Christian Gauls in dealing with pagan Franks one infers that his mission in Ireland preceded the

---

27 For evidence of the existence, duties, and status of *decuriones* in Roman Britain see R. G. Collingwood & R. P. Wright, *The Roman Inscriptions of Britain, I Inscriptions on Stone* (Oxford, 1965) 161 p. 53, 250 p. 82, 674 pp. 226-7, 812 p. 272; I. A. Richmond, *Roman Britain*, The Pelican History of England, ed. 2 (Harmondsworth, 1963, repr. 1967) pp. 88-90, 151, 184; A. L. F. Rivet, *Town and Country in Roman Britain*, rev. ed. (London, 1964, repr. 1966) pp. 64, 86, 113; J. Wacher, *The Towns of Roman Britain* (London, 1974, repr. 1983) 39-40, 43, 45, pl. 21, 135, pl. 24, 151, pl. 34, 172; P. Salway, *Roman Britain*, The Oxford History of England IA (Oxford, 1981, corr. repr. 1982) pp. 398, 575-6, 598, 604, 723, 727.

conversion of the Franks, traditionally in 496, but certainly before the death of Clovis in 511. Patrick's incidental references to coinage, *solidus* and *dimidium scriptulae*, are consistent with a period rather earlier than later, as archaeological sites imply that coins seem not to have circulated as currency in Britain long after the first quarter of the fifth century.[28]

If we infer from Patrick's diction for the periods of a lifetime the ordinary meanings, *infantia* for the first seven years, *pueritia* for years eight to fourteen, *adolescentia* for years fifteen to twenty-one, *iuuentus* for years twenty-two to forty-two, and *senectus* for the period after forty-two, we can learn something of the chronology of his career. He states in *Confessio* VIIII 19 (27) that he had not believed in the living God *ex infantia mea*. He committed a sin during his boyhood, *in pueritia mea*, probably when he was fourteen, *nescio ... si habebam tunc annos quindecim* VIIII 13, 16-7 (27). Within a year of that, when he was *adolescens immo paene puer inuerbis* VII 21 (10) he was captured, at the age of fifteen, *annorum eram tunc fere sedecim* I 9 (1), which he refers to again as *adolescentiae ... meae* I 24 (2). Because of the capture his education was interrupted. Patrick the *puer grammaticatus* did not become an *adolescens rhetoricatus*, but had instead to speak a foreign language during the six years of his captivity as a herdsman near the Forest of Foclut on the Atlantic coast of Ireland. After learning in a dream that he was about to return to his fatherland, Britain, not Gaul, he journeyed two hundred miles across Ireland, probably from northwest to southeast, whence he sailed for three days. After landing he and his travelling companions made a journey of *uiginti octo dies* 'twenty-eight days'. On *alio die*, the twenty-ninth day, the captain asked Patrick to ask his God for help, which arrived soon after Patrick's request. The company remained where they had found food two nights longer, *ibi duas noctes manserunt*, on the second of which, the thirty-first since landfall, Patrick experienced his great temptation by Satan. The pair to that story of the adventures of one month is an account of another capture, on the first night of which he dreamt that he would be with his captors for two months, *duobus mensibus eris cum illis*, which was fulfilled precisely, *nocte illa sexagesima liberauit me Dominus de manibus eorum*. Although this occurred many years afterwards, *post annos multos*, these passages show clearly that Patrick maintained a tight control over the chronology of his narrative.

If Patrick was fifteen at the time of his capture he was twenty-one at the time of his escape from Ireland and his return to Britain, where he had his vision of Victoricius bearing the letter with the *Uox Hiberionacum*, summoning him to evangelize the Irish. This occurred *in iuuentute*, to which Patrick refers four times: as a period during which he did not yet hope for grace great enough to do something like convert the Irish, *ego*

28 For a report of the largest hoard of Roman treasure ever found in Britain, including gold coins of Honorius, the last emperor to exercise authority in Roman Britain, see *The Independent*, 20 November 1992, pp. 1, 5.

aliquando in iuuentute mea numquam speraui neque cogitaui VII 85 (15); a period during which he did not acquire secular learning, *quod in iuuentute non comparaui* VII 17 (10); but also the time during which the love and fear of God grew in him, *ex quo cognoui eum a iuuentute mea creuit in me amor Dei et timor ipsius* XX 117-8 (44); and the time during which he began to live as a missionary among the Irish, *uos scitis et Deus qualiter inter uos conuersatus sum a iuuentute mea in fide ueritatis* XX 154-6 (48).

In the *Epistola* 23 (3) Patrick mentions a presbyter whom he had taught from infancy, *quem ego ex infantia docui*. As the normal age for ordination to the priesthood was thirty, one infers that by the time he composed that letter Patrick had been in Ireland for at least twenty-three years. Rejection of that letter sent with the presbyter elicited the letter of excommunication we know as the *Epistola ad Milites Corotici*. As Patrick states at the beginning of part **II** 40 (6) *Non usurpo* 'I am not claiming too much', one infers that his critics believed he was exceeding the limits of his authority. His attempt to excommunicate from Ireland a tyrant in Britain may have provoked the attack on his mission which he relates at the thematic crux of the *Confessio*.

The attack on Patrick's status as a bishop, *contra laboriosum episcopatum meum*, came from his ecclesiastical *seniores* in Britain during his absence. He states that he was abroad, once as a *peregrino* VIIII 5 (26) and again *quod ego non interfui nec in Brittanniis eram* XIIII 6-7 (32). They charged him generally with his sins, *peccata mea* (26), but specifically

> occasionem post annos triginta inuenerunt me aduersus
> uerbum quod confessus fueram antequam essem diaconus.

This sin, committed probably when he was fourteen, he confessed at least seven years later, before becoming a deacon, after his escape from Ireland, when he was twenty-one. As the *seniores* 'found out about' or 'invented' it thirty years later Patrick must have been at least fifty-one years old at the time of his ecclesiastical trial, well into his *senectus*. In the Apology written to defend himself from the *seniores* who tried him he states that he is *in senectute mea* VII 16 (10).

There are no loose threads in the account. Patrick probably believed that commission of the sin in boyhood was punished by his capture and enslavement the following year, which led to his spiritual awakening and his direct instruction through dream visions to undertake his mission to the Irish. As the sin was revealed by the *amicissimus* to whom it had been confessed, the attack on Patrick's episcopate came from the very man who had predicted his elevation to the episcopate. The attack on Patrick's fitness issued from an uncanonical revelation of a confessed sin. Patrick vindicates his claim to fitness with the account of his mission related in part **IIII**.

If we assume that Patrick was born about A.D. 390, his capture and enslavement occurred about the year 405 and his escape from Ireland about

411, in the general confusion following withdrawal of Roman civil and military administrators from Britain. Patrick can hardly have returned to Ireland as a missionary priest before the age of thirty, about 420. His elevation to the episcopate would follow later. Patrick nowhere states that he brought any ecclesiastical assistants with him from Britain, but he refers often to those converted, baptised, confirmed, ordained as clerics, and admitted to the religious life in Ireland. He can hardly have sent to Coroticus a priest whom he had taught in Ireland *ex infantia* before 443. Patrick's attempt as a bishop *Hiberione constitutus* to excommunicate from Ireland a tyrant in Britain may have provoked British ecclesiastical authorities to try and condemn him in his absence. Patrick may have responded by proceeding without their approval to some great or dramatic act.

Since Binchy's witty and withering critical assessment of St Patrick and his biographers ancient and modern it has been fashionable to distrust the Irish annals of events of the fifth century. But the dates suggested above are not inconsistent with the testimony of the *Annals of Ulster* that A.D. 432 *Patricius peruenit ad Hiberniam*, 441 *probatus est in fide catolica Patricius episcopus*, 443 *Patricius episcopus ardore fidei et doctrina Christi florens in nostra prouincia*, 444 *Ard Macha fundata est*, and 461 *Hic alii quietem Patrici dicunt*, that is in about his seventy-second year. The annal 491 *Dicunt scoiti hic Patricium archiepiscopum defunctum* would imply death in about his hundredth year.

A question more easily answered than the date of Patrick's death is this: should one suspect the foregoing analyses as violent manipulation or sleight of hand by the present writer, or respect them as designs composed deliberately and systematically by the author to ensure accurate transmission of texts and to assist comprehension of explicit and implicit meanings? If these analyses of primary Patrician texts are even approximately correct they entail revision of many inferences drawn in the secondary and tertiary Patrician literature.

The most misleading opinion to be changed is that Patrick was an inarticulate artless man of simple piety burdened by a sense of his educational and intellectual inferiority. One may hope never again to be told that 'Patrick certainly ... thought less of himself than of anybody else'[29] or

> The root trait in Patrick's character is a sense of helplessness, of being vulnerable. ... But Patrick had another cause for the strong sense of inadequacy which shows itself constantly in his writing: the deficiencies of his education'.[30]
>
> His Latin prose ... is destitute of any artificial rhetoric whatever. This is what gives his prose its clumsiness but also its note of sincerity and its directness of appeal.[31]

29 Bieler, *Life and Legend* p. 49.
30 Hanson, *Life and Writings* pp. 36-7.
31 *Idem, Patrick Origins* p. 111.

We need not doubt Patrick's humility before God. Anyone who believes that he has seen and heard the Spirit of the eternal, omnipotent, omniscient Creator of the universe inside his own body praying over his interior man will retain for the rest of his life a proper sense of his creaturely finiteness. But if he believes that God has joined him to Himself he will not necessarily feel inferior to his fellow men. Nor did Patrick. When he writes in the *Epistola* that he is *indoctus* he is not lamenting that he is 'unlearned'. He is boasting that he is 'untaught' by men, proclaiming his status as a bishop, and affirming that his authority derives directly from God, *Certissime reor a Deo accepi id quod sum*. Similarly in the *Confessio* in his Apology he is by no means regretting the lack of rhetorical finish. For twenty clauses in succession he flaunts his ability not only to compose *clausulae* but to arrange them in patterns by type. Having shown once that he can do this, he never does it again, but goes into attack. When he writes that he has not learned 'like the others' the context of his quotation implies that 'the others' are not Christians. When he appears to concede that they pursued their learning 'to perfection' the context of his quotation implies that such pursuit brings no one to perfection. When he addresses the *domini cati rethorici* directly the chiastic structure of his prose implies that they are distinct from the 'great and small who fear God'. By judicious arrangement of word order he changes St Paul's address to his converts, 'You are the letter of Christ', to 'I am the letter of Christ', using the non-inclusive royal 'we', but with his third person verb *inquit* still attributing the claim to St Paul. After consecutively applying to himself the words of Moses, Isaiah, St Paul, St Luke, and Jesus ben Sirach, and arrogating to himself the authority of Lawgiver, Prophet, Apostle, and Evangelist, while simultaneously using the unquoted context of his quotations to attack his critics, he proclaims as the crown of his argument that what his critics regard as a defect is actually a divinely appointed virtue, *Spiritus testatur Et rusticationem ab Altissimo creatam*. This is not the behaviour of a modest man with a sense of his own inferiority. It is the indignation, the outrage, of a man who knows that his own sense of worth and dignity is not shared by others. Imagine a member of an ethnic or cultural minority historically disadvantaged in our society, say a self-possessed black or gay man confronting an unreconstructed straight white Anglo-Saxon Protestant man, a strong policewoman responding to attempted sexual harassment, or a female university lecturer reacting to perceived condescension from someone who is expecting deference and not receiving it. Not a situation in which to expect conventionally 'nice' behaviour. We may suppose similarly that St Patrick was not a 'nice' man, any more than his hero St Paul was an easy person to deal with. We should not suppose that he was hampered by a sense of inadequacy.

One of the effects of Binchy's critique has been to separate the later tradition from the works of St Patrick, leaving readers to wonder how the hagiographers, a gaggle of propagandists and liars, converted the 'simple Patrick of the Confessio' into 'the glorified Patrick of the biographies', a sort of druid, ready to curse, blast, blind, and maim anyone who crossed him, even to drive a chariot over St Sechnall. One answer, which emerges from the present analysis, is that mediaeval writers understood more clearly than modern critics the self-confident undertones and implications of Patrick's prose. They recognized as aggressive self-assertion, or even provocation, what modern men have mistaken as anguished self-deprecation. By reading, as suggested above, Patrick's and the hagiographers' works together, one repairs the apparent disjuncture between the saint's own writings and the later tradition. One is not obliged to believe everything they tell us, but one is advised to look in their works as in his for comprehension and art where our predecessors have been prone to suspect misprision and disorder, quick to apply inappropriate criteria for aesthetic judgement, and ready to adapt the perceived mess to their own purposes.

In the work of modern scholars, if we consider only the finest — Bieler, Carney, Binchy, and Hanson — we find misjudgements about Patrick so gross as to imply that these men were using the saint's writings as a script for their own psycho-historical analyses, a remote field on which to wage personal battles and work out animosities and partisan agendas. Even here it may be that Patrick's irascibility has evoked across the centuries something deep and dark and aggressive in our contemporaries, part of his *exagalliae* to his heirs. There remain nonetheless immense riches in the philological learning of Bieler, the brilliant imaginative intuition of Carney, the critical acumen and wit of Binchy, and the dispassionate judgement and learning of Hanson that no one would wisely forego. That also is part of Patrick's *exagalliae* to us.

If any work is to be more than ephemeral it must be received in contexts not foreseen and interpreted in ways not intended by its maker. The more contexts into which a work can be fitted the more likely it is to be transmitted across centuries. The works of St Patrick have been received, interpreted, and adapted by his heirs in many centuries in varied ways. The purpose of the present book is not to survey that tradition of reception, but to suggest that the primary texts exhibit features inbuilt to guarantee the integrity and authenticity of the author's words, to aid our comprehension of his meanings, to delight and engage and instruct us. The works of St Patrick are the oldest extant Latin texts written in these islands by a native of these islands for inhabitants of these islands. In his words and patterns of thought and literary structures Patrick illustrates the reception and assimilation of an ancient Biblical tradition, which became through him the very foundation of our tradition. Now fifteen centuries old, it retains, as it has never lost, the power to enrich both our personal and our common life.

EPISTOLA AD MILITES COROTICI AND CONFESSIO PLAIN TEXTS

LIBER EPISTOLARUM SANCTI PATRICII EPISCOPI

I. EPISTOLA AD MILITES COROTICI

Patricius peccator indoctus scilicet Hiberione constitutus episcopum me esse fateor. Certissime reor a Deo 'accepi id quod sum'. Inter barbaras itaque gentes habito proselitus et profuga ob amorem Dei; testis est ille si ita est. Non quod optabam tam dure et tam aspere aliquid ex ore meo effundere, sed cogor zelo Dei et ueritas Xpisti excitauit, pro dilectione proximorum atque filiorum, pro quibus 'tradidi' patriam et parentes et 'animam meam usque ad mortem'. Si dignus sum uiuo Deo meo docere gentes etsi contempnor aliquibus. Manu mea scripsi atque condidi uerba ista danda et tradenda militibus mittenda Corotici, non dico ciuibus meis neque ciuibus sanctorum Romanorum sed ciuibus daemoniorum ob mala opera ipsorum. Ritu hostili in morte uiuunt, socii Scottorum atque Pictorum apostatarumque, sanguilentos sanguinare de sanguine innocentium Xpistianorum, 'quos' ego innumerum numerum Deo 'genui' atque 'in Xpisto' confirmaui. Postera die qua crismati neophyti in ueste candida — flagrabat in fronte ipsorum dum crudeliter trucidati atque mactati gladio supradictis — misi epistolam cum sancto presbytero quem ego ex infantia docui cum clericis ut nobis aliquid indulgerent de praeda uel de captiuis baptizatis quos ceperunt: cachinnos fecerunt de illis. Idcirco nescio quid magis lugeam: an qui interfecti uel quos ceperunt uel quos grauiter zabulus inlaqueauit. Perenni poena gehennam pariter cum ipso mancipabunt quia utique 'qui facit peccatum seruus est' et 'filius zabuli' nuncupatur. Quapropter resciat omnis homo timens Deum quod a me alieni sunt et a Xpisto Deo meo 'pro quo legationem fungor', patricida, fratricida, 'lupi rapaces deuorantes plebem Domini ut cibum panis', sicut ait 'Iniqui dissipauerunt legem tuam, Domine', quam in supremis temporibus Hiberione optime benigne plantauerat atque instructa erat fauente Deo.

Non usurpo. Partem habeo cum his 'quos aduocauit et praedestinauit' euangelium praedicare in persecutionibus non paruis 'usque ad extremum terrae', etsi inuidet inimicus per tyrannidem Corotici, qui Deum non ueretur nec sacerdotes ipsius, quos elegit et indulsit illis summam diuinam sublimam potestatem, 'quos ligarent super terram ligatos esse et in caelis'. Unde ergo quaeso plurimum 'sancti et humiles corde' adulari talibus non licet 'nec cibum' nec potum 'sumere' cum ipsis nec elemosinas ipsorum recipi debeat donec crudeliter paenitentiam effusis lacrimis satis Deo faciant et liberent seruos Dei et ancillas Xpisti baptizatas, pro quibus mortuus est et crucifixus. 'Dona iniquorum reprobat Altissimus.' 'Qui offert sacrificium ex substantia pauperum quasi qui uictimat filium in conspectu patris sui.' 'Diuitias' inquit 'quas congregauit iniuste euomentur de uentre eius, trahit illum angelus mortis, ira draconum mulcabitur, interficiet illum lingua colubris, comedit autem eum ignis inextinguibilis' ideoque 'Uae qui replent se quae non sunt sua', uel 'Quid prodest homini ut totum mundum lucretur et animae suae detrimentum patiatur?' Longum est per singula discutere uel insinuare, per totam legem carpere testimonia de tali cupiditate. Auaritia mortale crimen. 'Non concupisces rem proximi tui. Non occides.' Homicida non potest esse cum Xpisto. 'Qui odit fratrem suum homicida' adscribitur uel 'Qui non diligit fratrem suum in morte manet'. Quanto magis reus est qui manus suas coinquinauit in sanguine filiorum Dei, quos nuper 'adquisiuit' in ultimis terrae per exhortationem paruitatis nostrae?

Numquid sine Deo uel 'secundum carnem' Hiberione ueni? Quis me compulit? 'Alligatus' sum 'Spiritu' ut non uideam aliquem 'de cognatione mea'. Numquid a me piam misericordiam quod ago erga gentem illam qui me aliquando ceperunt et deuastauerunt seruos et ancillas domus patris mei? Ingenuus fui 'secundum carnem'; decurione patre nascor. Uendidi enim nobilitatem meam — non erubesco neque me paenitet — pro utilitate aliorum; denique seruus sum in Xpisto genti exterae ob gloriam ineffabilem 'perennis uitae quae est in Xpisto Iesu Domino nostro'. Et si mei me non cognoscunt 'propheta in patria sua honorem non habet'. Forte non sumus 'ex uno ouili' neque 'unum Deum patrem' habemus, sicut ait 'Qui non est mecum contra me est et qui non congregat mecum spargit'. Non conuenit: 'Unus destruit, alter aedificat.' 'Non quaero quae mea sunt.' Non mea gratia sed Deus 'qui dedit hanc sollicitudinem in corde meo' ut unus essem de 'uenatoribus siue piscatoribus' quos olim Deus 'in nouissimis diebus' ante praenuntiauit. Inuidetur mihi. Quid faciam, Domine? Ualde despicior. Ecce oues tuae circa me laniantur atque depraedantur et supradictis latrunculis iubente Corotico hostili mente. Longe est a caritate Dei traditor Xpistianorum in manus Scottorum atque Pictorum. 'Lupi rapaces' deglutierunt gregem Domini, qui utique Hiberione cum summa diligentia optime crescebat, et filii Scottorum et filiae regulorum monachi et uirgines Xpisti enumerare nequeo. Quam ob rem 'iniuria iustorum non te placeat'; etiam 'usque ad inferos non placebit'. Quis sanctorum non horreat iocundare uel conuiuium fruere cum talibus? De spoliis defunctorum Xpistianorum repleuerunt domos suas, de rapinis uiuunt. Nesciunt miseri uenenum letale cibum porrigunt ad amicos et filios suos, sicut Eua non intellexit quod utique mortem tradidit uiro suo. Sic sunt omnes qui male agunt: 'mortem' perennem poenam 'operantur'. Consuetudo Romanorum Gallorum Xpistianorum: mittunt uiros sanctos idoneos ad Francos et ceteras gentes cum tot milia solidorum ad redimendos captiuos baptizatos. Tu potius interficis et uendis illos genti exterae ignoranti Deum; quasi in lupanar tradis 'membra Xpisti'. Qualem spem habes in Deum uel qui te consentit aut qui te communicat uerbis adulationis? Deus iudicabit. Scriptum est enim 'Non solum facientes mala sed etiam consentientes damnandi sunt.' Nescio 'quid dicam' uel 'quid loquar' amplius de defunctis filiorum Dei, quos gladius supra modum dure tetigit. Scriptum est enim 'Flete cum flentibus' et iterum 'Si dolet unum membrum condoleant omnia membra'. Quapropter ecclesia 'plorat et plangit filios' et filias 'suas' quas adhuc gladius nondum interfecit, sed prolongati et exportati in longa terrarum, ubi 'peccatum' manifeste grauiter impudenter 'abundat', ibi uenundati ingenui homines, Xpistiani in seruitute redacti sunt, praesertim indignissimorum pessimorum apostatarumque Pictorum. Idcirco cum tristitia et maerore uociferabo: O speciosissimi atque amantissimi fratres et filii 'quos in Xpisto genui' enumerare nequeo, quid faciam uobis? Non sum dignus Deo neque hominibus subuenire. 'Praeualuit iniquitas iniquorum super nos.' Quasi 'extranei facti sumus'. Forte non credunt 'unum baptismum' percepimus uel 'unum Deum patrem' habemus. Indignum est illis Hiberionaci sumus. Sicut ait 'Nonne unum Deum habetis?' 'Quid dereliquistis unusquisque proximum suum?'

Idcirco doleo pro uobis, doleo, carissimi mihi; sed iterum gaudeo intra meipsum: non gratis 'laboraui' uel peregrinatio mea 'in uacuum' non fuit. Et contigit scelus tam horrendum ineffabile, Deo gratias, creduli baptizati, de saeculo recessistis ad paradisum. Cerno uos: migrare coepistis ubi 'nox non erit' 'neque luctus neque mors amplius', 'sed exultabitis sicut uituli ex uinculis resoluti et conculcabitis iniquos et erunt cinis sub pedibus uestris'. Uos ergo regnabitis cum apostolis et prophetis atque martyribus. Aeterna regna capietis, sicut ipse testatur inquit 'Uenient ab oriente et occidente et recumbent cum Abraham et Isaac et Iacob in regno caelorum. Foris canes et uenefici et homicidae' et 'Mendacibus periuris pars eorum in stagnum ignis aeterni.' Non inmerito ait apostolus 'Ubi iustus uix saluus erit peccator et impius transgressor legis ubi se recognoscet?' Unde enim Coroticus cum suis sceleratissimis, rebellatores Xpisti, ubi se uidebunt, qui mulierculas baptizatas praemia distribuunt ob miserum regnum temporale, quod utique in momento transeat? 'Sicut nubes uel fumus, qui utique uento dispergitur', ita 'peccatores' fraudulenti 'a facie Domini peribunt; iusti autem epulentur in magna constantia' cum Xpisto 'iudicabunt nationes et' regibus iniquis 'dominabuntur' in saecula saeculorum. Amen. 'Testificor coram Deo et angelis suis' quod ita erit sicut intimauit imperitiae meae. Non mea uerba sed Dei et apostolorum atque prophetarum quod ego Latinum exposui, qui numquam enim mentiti sunt. 'Qui crediderit saluus erit, qui uero non crediderit condempnabitur, Deus locutus est.' Quaeso plurimum ut quicumque famulus Dei promptus fuerit ut sit gerulus litterarum harum, ut nequaquam subtrahatur uel abscondatur a nemine, sed magis potius legatur coram cunctis plebibus et praesente ipso Corotico. Quod si Deus inspirat illos 'ut quandoque Deo resipiscant', ita ut uel sero paeniteant quod tam impie gesserunt — homicida erga fratres Domini — et liberent captiuas baptizatas quas ante ceperunt, ita ut mereantur Deo uiuere et sani efficiantur hic et in aeternum. Pax Patri et Filio et Spiritui Sancto. Amen.

II. CONFESSIO

Ego Patricius peccator rusticissimus et minimus omnium fidelium et contemptibilissimus apud plurimos patrem habui Calpornium diaconum filium quendam Potiti presbyteri, qui fuit uico Bannauenta Berniae; uillulam enim prope habuit, ubi ego capturam dedi. Annorum eram tunc fere sedecim. Deum enim uerum ignorabam et Hiberione in captiuitate adductus sum cum tot milia hominum secundum merita nostra, quia 'a Deo recessimus' et 'praecepta eius non custodiuimus' et sacerdotibus nostris non oboedientes fuimus, qui nostram salutem admonebant, et Deus 'induxit super nos iram animationis suae et dispersit nos in gentibus' multis etiam 'usque ad ultimum terrae', ubi nunc paruitas mea esse uidetur inter alienigenas, et ibi 'Dominus aperuit sensum incredulitatis meae' ut uel sero rememorarem delicta mea et ut 'conuerterem toto corde ad Dominum Deum meum', qui 'respexit humilitatem meam' et misertus est adolescentiae et ignorantiae meae et custodiuit me antequam scirem eum et antequam saperem uel distinguerem inter bonum et malum et muniuit me et consolatus est me ut pater filium.

Unde autem tacere non possum 'neque expedit quidem' tanta beneficia et tantam gratiam quam mihi Dominus praestare dignatus est 'in terra captiuitatis meae', quia haec est retributio nostra, ut post correptionem uel agnitionem Dei 'exaltare et confiteri mirabilia eius coram omni natione quae est sub omni caelo'.

Quia non est alius Deus nec umquam fuit ante nec erit post haec praeter Deum Patrem ingenitum, sine principio, a quo est omne principium, omnia tenentem, ut didicimus, et huius filium Iesum Xpistum, quem cum Patre scilicet semper fuisse testamur, ante originem saeculi spiritaliter apud Patrem inenarrabiliter genitum ante omne principium, et per ipsum facta sunt uisibilia et inuisibilia, hominem factum, morte deuicta in caelis ad Patrem receptum, 'et dedit illi omnem potestatem super omne nomen caelestium et terrestrium et infernorum et omnis lingua confiteatur ei quia Dominus et Deus est Iesus Xpistus', quem credimus et expectamus aduentum ipsius mox futurum, 'iudex uiuorum atque mortuorum, qui reddet unicuique secundum facta sua': et 'effudit in nobis abunde Spiritum Sanctum, donum' et 'pignus' inmortalitatis, qui facit credentes et oboedientes ut sint 'filii Dei' et 'coheredes Xpisti', quem confitemur et adoramus unum Deum in Trinitate sacri nominis.

Ipse enim dixit per prophetam 'Inuoca me in die tribulationis tuae et liberabo te et magnificabis me'. Et iterum inquit 'Opera autem Dei reuelare et confiteri honorificum est'.

Tamen etsi in multis imperfectus sum opto 'fratribus et cognatis' meis scire qualitatem meam, ut possint perspicere uotum animae meae.

Non ignoro 'testimonium Domini mei', qui in psalmo testatur 'Perdes eos qui loquuntur mendacium'. Et iterum inquit 'Os quod mentitur occidit animam'. Et idem Dominus in euangelio inquit 'Uerbum otiosum quod locuti fuerint homines reddent pro eo rationem in die iudicii'. Unde autem uehementer debueram 'cum timore et tremore' metuere hanc sententiam in die illa ubi nemo se poterit subtrahere uel abscondere, sed omnes omnino 'reddituri sumus rationem' etiam minimorum peccatorum 'ante tribunal Domini Xpisti'.

Quapropter olim cogitaui scribere, sed et 'usque nunc' haesitaui; timui enim ne 'inciderem in linguam' hominum, quia non didici 'sicut' et 'ceteri', qui optime itaque iura et sacras litteras utraque pari modo combiberunt et sermones illorum ex infantia numquam mutarunt, sed magis 'ad perfectum' semper addiderunt. Nam 'sermo et loquela' nostra translata est in linguam alienam, sicut facile potest probari ex saliua scripturae meae qualiter 'sum ego' in sermonibus instructus atque 'eruditus', quia, inquit, 'Sapiens per linguam dinoscetur et sensus et scientia et doctrina ueritatis'. Sed quid prodest excusatio 'iuxta ueritatem', praesertim cum praesumptione, quatenus modo ipse adpeto 'in senectute' mea quod 'in iuuentute' non comparaui, quod obstiterunt peccata mea ut confirmarem quod ante perlegeram. Sed quis me credit etsi dixero quod ante praefatus sum?

Adolescens, immo paene puer inuerbis, capturam dedi, antequam scirem quid adpetere uel quid uitare debueram. Unde ergo hodie erubesco et uehementer pertimeo denudare imperitiam meam, quia disertis breuitate 'sermone explicare' nequeo, sicut enim spiritus gestit et animus, et sensus monstrat adfectus. Sed si itaque datum mihi fuisset 'sicut' et 'ceteris' uerumtamen non silerem 'propter retributionem'.

Et si forte uidetur apud aliquantos me in hoc praeponere cum mea inscientia et 'tardiori lingua', sed etiam scriptum est enim 'Linguae balbutientes uelociter discent loqui pacem'. Quanto magis nos adpetere debemus, qui sumus, inquit, 'epistola Xpisti in salutem usque ad ultimum terrae', et si non diserta sed rata et fortissima, 'scripta in cordibus uestris non atramento sed spiritu Dei uiui'. Et iterum Spiritus testatur 'Et rusticationem ab Altissimo creatam'.

Unde ego primus rusticus profuga indoctus scilicet, 'qui nescio in posterum prouidere', sed illud 'scio certissime quia' utique 'priusquam humiliarer' ego eram uelut lapis qui iacet in 'luto profundo': et uenit 'qui potens est' et in 'sua misericordia' sustulit me et quidem scilicet sursum adleuauit et collocauit me in summo pariete, et inde fortiter debueram exclamare 'ad retribuendum' quoque aliquid 'Domino' pro tantis beneficiis eius hic et in aeternum, quae mens hominum aestimare non potest.

Unde autem admiramini itaque 'magni et pusilli qui timetis Deum' et uos domini cati rethorici audite ergo et scrutamini quis me stultum excitauit de medio eorum qui uidentur esse sapientes et legis periti et 'potentes in sermone' et in omni re, et me quidem, detestabilis huius mundi, prae ceteris inspirauit si talis essem — dummodo autem — ut 'cum metu et reuerentia' et 'sine querella' fideliter prodessem genti ad quam 'caritas Xpisti' transtulit et donauit me in uita mea, si dignus fuero, denique ut cum humilitate et ueraciter deseruirem illis. In 'mensura' itaque 'fidei' Trinitatis oportet distinguere sine reprehensione periculi notum facere 'donum Dei' et 'consolationem aeternam', sine timore fiducialiter Dei nomen ubique expandere, ut etiam 'post obitum meum' exagallias relinquere fratribus et filiis meis quos in Domino ego baptizaui tot milia hominum, et non eram dignus neque talis ut hoc Dominus seruulo suo concederet, post aerumnas et tantas moles, post captiuitatem, post annos multos in gentem illam tantam gratiam mihi donaret, quod ego aliquando in iuuentute mea numquam speraui neque cogitaui.

Sed postquam Hiberione deueneram cotidie itaque pecora pascebam et frequens in die orabam, magis ac magis accedebat amor Dei et timor ipsius et fides augebatur et spiritus agebatur, ut in die una usque ad centum orationes et in nocte prope similiter, ut etiam in siluis et monte manebam, et ante lucem excitabar ad orationem per niuem, per gelu, per pluuiam, et nihil mali sentiebam neque ulla pigritia erat in me, sicut modo uideo, quia tunc spiritus in me feruebat, et ibi scilicet quadam nocte in somno audiui uocem dicentem mihi "Bene ieiunas cito iturus ad patriam tuam", et iterum post paululum tempus audiui 'responsum' dicentem mihi "Ecce nauis tua parata est" et non erat prope, sed forte habebat ducenta milia passus et ibi numquam fueram nec ibi notum quemquam de hominibus habebam, et deinde postmodum con-uersus sum in fugam et intermisi hominem cum quo fueram sex annis et ueni in uirtute Dei, qui uiam meam ad bonum dirigebat et nihil metuebam donec perueni ad nauem illam, et illa die qua perueni profecta est nauis de loco suo, et locutus sum ut haberem unde nauigare cum illis et gubernator displicuit illi et acriter cum indignatione respondit "Nequaquam tu nobiscum adpetes ire" et cum haec audiissem separaui me ab illis ut uenirem ad teguriolum ubi hospitabam, et in itinere coepi orare et antequam orationem consummarem audiui unum ex illis et fortiter exclamabat post me "Ueni cito, quia uocant te homines isti", et statim ad illos reuersus sum, et coeperunt mihi dicere "Ueni, quia ex fide recipimus te; fac nobiscum amicitiam quo modo uolueris" et in illa die itaque reppuli 'sugere mammellas eorum' propter timorem Dei, sed uerumtamen ab illis speraui uenire in fidem Iesu Xpisti, quia gentes erant, et ob hoc obtinui cum illis, et protinus nauigauimus.

Et post triduum terram cepimus et uiginti octo dies per desertum iter fecimus et cibus defuit illis et 'fames inualuit super eos', et alio die coepit gubernator mihi dicere "Quid est, Xpistiane? Tu dicis Deus tuus magnus et omnipotens est; quare ergo non potes pro nobis orare, quia nos a fame periclitamur; difficile est enim ut aliquem hominem umquam uideamus." Ego enim confidenter dixi illis "'Conuertemini' ex fide 'ex toto corde ad Dominum Deum meum, quia nihil est impossibile illi', ut hodie cibum mittat uobis in uiam uestram usque dum satiamini, quia ubique abundabat illi".

Et adiuuante Deo ita factum est: ecce grex porcorum in uia ante oculos nostros apparuit, et multos ex illis interfecerunt et ibi duas noctes manserunt et bene refecti et carne eorum repleti sunt, quia multi ex illis 'defecerunt' et secus uiam 'semiuiui relicti' sunt, et post hoc summas gratias egerunt Deo et ego honorificatus sum sub oculis eorum, et ex hac die cibum abundanter habuerunt; etiam 'mel siluestre' inuenerunt et 'mihi partem obtulerunt' et unus ex illis dixit "'Immolaticium est'". Deo gratias exinde nihil gustaui.

Eadem uero nocte eram dormiens et fortiter temptauit me Satanas, quod memor ero 'quamdiu fuero in hoc corpore', et cecidit super me ueluti saxum ingens et nihil membrorum meorum praeualens. Sed unde me uenit ignaro in spiritu ut Heliam uocarem? Et inter haec uidi in caelum solem oriri et dum clamarem "Helia, Helia" uiribus meis, ecce splendor solis illius decidit super me et statim discussit a me omnem grauitudinem, et credo quod a Xpisto Domino meo subuentus sum et Spiritus eius iam tunc clamabat pro me et spero quod sic erit 'in die pressurae' meae, sicut in euangelio inquit 'In illa die', Dominus testatur, 'non uos estis qui loquimini, sed Spiritus Patris uestri qui loquitur in uobis'.

Et iterum post annos multos adhuc capturam dedi. Ea nocte prima itaque mansi cum illis. 'Responsum' autem 'diuinum' audiui dicentem mihi "Duobus mensibus eris cum illis". Quod ita factum est: nocte illa sexagesima 'liberauit me Dominus de manibus eorum'.

Etiam in itinere praeuidit nobis cibum et ignem et siccitatem cotidie donec decimo die peruenimus homines. Sicut superius insinuaui, uiginti et octo dies per desertum iter fecimus et ea nocte qua peruenimus homines de cibo uero nihil habuimus.

Et iterum post paucos annos in Brittanniis eram cum parentibus meis, qui me ut filium susceperunt et ex fide rogauerunt me ut uel modo ego post tantas tribulationes quas ego pertuli nusquam ab illis discederem, et ibi scilicet 'uidi in uisu noctis' uirum uenientem quasi de Hiberione, cui nomen Uictoricius, cum epistolis innumerabilibus, et dedit mihi unam ex his et legi principium epistolae continentem 'Uox Hiberionacum', et cum recitabam principium epistolae putabam ipso momento audire uocem ipsorum qui erant iuxta siluam Uocluti quae est prope mare occidentale, et sic exclamauerunt 'quasi ex uno ore' "Rogamus te, sancte puer, ut uenias et adhuc ambulas inter nos" et ualde 'compunctus sum corde' et amplius non potui legere et sic expertus sum. Deo gratias, quia post plurimos annos praestitit illis Dominus secundum clamorem illorum.

Et alia nocte, 'nescio, Deus scit', utrum in me an iuxta me, uerbis peritissimis, quos ego audiui et non potui intellegere, nisi ad postremum orationis sic effitiatus est '"Qui dedit animam suam pro te' ipse est qui loquitur in te" et sic expergefactus sum gaudibundus. Et iterum uidi in me ipsum orantem et eram quasi intra corpus meum et audiui super me, hoc est super 'interiorem hominem', et ibi fortiter orabat gemitibus, et inter haec 'stupebam et admirabam et cogitabam' quis esset qui in me orabat, sed ad postremum orationis sic effitiatus est ut sit Spiritus, et sic expertus sum et recordatus sum apostolo dicente 'Spiritus adiuuat infirmitates orationis nostrae: nam quod oremus sicut oportet nescimus, sed ipse Spiritus postulat pro nobis gemitibus inenarrabilibus, quae uerbis exprimi non possunt'; et iterum 'Dominus aduocatus noster postulat pro nobis'.

Et quando temptatus sum ab aliquantis senioribus meis, qui uenerunt et peccata mea contra laboriosum episcopatum meum obiecerunt, utique illo die fortiter 'impulsus sum ut caderem' hic et in aeternum; sed Dominus pepercit proselito et peregrino propter nomen suum benigne et ualde mihi subuenit in hac conculcatione. Quod in labe et in obprobrium non male deueni. Deum oro ut 'non illis in peccatum reputetur'. 'Occasionem' post annos triginta 'inuenerunt me aduersus' uerbum quod confessus fueram antequam essem diaconus. Propter anxietatem maesto animo insinuaui amicissimo meo quae in pueritia mea una die gesseram, immo in una hora, quia necdum praeualebam. 'Nescio, Deus scit', si habebam tunc annos quindecim, et Deum uiuum non credebam neque ex infantia mea, sed in morte et in incredulitate mansi donec ualde castigatus sum 'et in ueritate humiliatus sum a fame et nuditate' et cotidie.

Contra, Hiberione non sponte pergebam 'donec' prope 'deficiebam'; sed hoc potius bene mihi fuit, qui ex hoc emendatus sum a Domino et aptauit me ut hodie essem quod aliquando longe a me erat, ut ego curam haberem aut satagerem pro salute aliorum quando autem tunc etiam de me ipso non cogitabam.

Igitur in illo die quo 'reprobatus sum' a memoratis supradictis ad noctem illam 'uidi in uisu noctis' quod scriptum erat contra faciem meam sine honore, et inter haec audiui 'responsum diuinum' dicentem mihi "Male uidimus faciem designati nudato nomine", nec sic praedixit "male uidisti" sed "male uidimus" quasi sibi me iunxisset sicut dixit 'Qui uos tangit quasi qui tangit pupillam oculi mei'.

Idcirco 'gratias ago ei qui me' in omnibus 'confortauit', ut non me impediret a profectione quam statueram et de mea quoque opera quod a Xpisto Domino meo didiceram, sed magis ex eo 'sensi in me uirtutem' non paruam et fides mea probata est coram Deo et hominibus.

Unde autem 'audenter dico' non me reprehendit conscientia mea hic et in futurum: 'teste Deo' habeo 'quia non sum mentitus' in sermonibus quos ego retuli uobis.

Sed magis doleo pro amicissimo meo cur hoc meruimus audire tale responsum. Cui ego credidi etiam animam. Et comperi ab aliquantis fratribus ante defensionem illam, quod ego non interfui nec in Brittanniis eram nec a me oriebatur, ut et ille in mea absentia pulsaret pro me; etiam mihi ipse ore suo dixerat "Ecce dandus es tu ad gradum episcopatus", quod non eram dignus. Sed unde uenit illi postmodum ut coram cunctis, bonis et malis, et me publice dehonestaret quod ante sponte et laetus indulserat, et Dominus, qui 'maior omnibus est'?

Satis 'dico'. Sed tamen non debeo abscondere 'donum Dei' quod largitus est nobis 'in terra captiuitatis meae', quia tunc fortiter inquisiui eum et ibi inueni illum et seruauit me ab omnibus iniquitatibus, sic credo, 'propter inhabitantem Spiritum' eius, qui 'operatus est' usque in hanc diem in me. 'Audenter' rursus. Sed scit Deus si mihi homo hoc effatus fuisset, forsitan tacuissem propter 'caritatem Xpisti'.

Unde ergo indefessam gratiam ago Deo meo qui me fidelem seruauit 'in die temptationis' meae, ita ut hodie confidenter offeram illi sacrificium ut 'hostiam uiuentem' animam meam Xpisto Domino meo, qui me 'seruauit ab omnibus angustiis meis' ut et dicam 'Quis ego sum, Domine', uel quae est uocatio mea, qui mihi tanta diuinitate comparuisti, ita ut hodie 'in gentibus' constanter 'exaltarem et magnificarem nomen tuum' ubicumque loco fuero, nec non in secundis sed etiam in pressuris, ut quicquid mihi euenerit siue bonum siue malum aequaliter debeo suscipere et Deo gratias semper agere, qui mihi ostendit ut indubitabilem eum sine fine crederem et qui me audierit ut ego inscius et 'in nouissimis diebus' hoc opus tam pium et tam mirificum auderem adgredere, ita ut imitarem quippiam illos quos ante Dominus iam olim praedixerat praenuntiaturos euangelium suum 'in testimonium omnibus gentibus' ante 'finem mundi', quod ita ergo uidimus itaque suppletum est. Ecce testes sumus quia euangelium praedicatum est usque ubi nemo ultra est.

Longum est autem totum per singula enarrare laborem meum uel per partes. Breuiter dicam qualiter piissimus Deus de seruitute saepe liberauit et de periculis duodecim qua periclitata est anima mea praeter insidias multas et 'quae uerbis exprimere non ualeo'. Nec iniuriam legentibus faciam, sed Deum auctorem habeo, qui nouit omnia etiam antequam fiant, ut me pauperculum pupillum idiotam 'responsum diuinum' crebre admonere.

'Unde mihi haec sapientia', quae in me non erat, qui nec 'numerum dierum noueram' neque Deum sapiebam? Unde mihi postmodum donum tam magnum tam salubre Deum agnoscere uel diligere, sed ut patriam et parentes amitterem?

Et munera multa mihi offerebantur cum fletu et lacrimis et offendi illos, nec non contra uotum aliquantos de senioribus meis, sed gubernante Deo nullo modo consensi neque adquieui illis, non mea gratia, sed Deus qui uincit in me et resistit illis omnibus, ut ego ueneram ad Hibernas gentes euangelium praedicare et ab incredulis contumelias perferre, ut 'audirem obprobrium peregrinationis meae', et persecutiones multas 'usque ad uincula' et ut darem ingenuitatem meam pro utilitate aliorum et, si dignus fuero, 'promptus' sum ut etiam 'animam meam' incunctanter et 'libentissime' pro nomine eius.

Et ibi opto 'impendere' eam 'usque ad mortem' si Dominus mihi indulgeret, quia ualde 'debitor sum' Deo, qui mihi tantam gratiam donauit ut populi multi per me in Deum renascerentur et postmodum consummarentur et ut clerici ubique illis ordinarentur ad plebem nuper uenientem ad credulitatem, quam sumpsit Dominus 'ab extremis terrae', sicut olim promiserat per prophetas suos: 'Ad te gentes uenient ab extremis terrae et dicent, "Sicut falsa comparauerunt patres nostri idola et non est in eis utilitas"' et iterum 'Posui te lumen in gentibus ut sis in salutem usque ad extremum terrae'. Et ibi uolo 'expectare promissum' ipsius, qui utique numquam fallit, sicut in euangelio pollicetur: 'Uenient ab oriente et occidente et recumbent cum Abraham et Isaac et Iacob', sicut credimus ab omni mundo uenturi sunt credentes. Idcirco itaque oportet quidem bene et diligenter piscare, sicut Dominus praemonet et docet dicens: 'Uenite post me et faciam uos fieri piscatores hominum' et iterum dicit per prophetas: 'Ecce mitto piscatores et uenatores multos, dicit Deus' et cetera. Unde autem ualde oportebat retia nostra tendere, ita ut 'multitudo copiosa et turba' Deo caperetur et ubique essent clerici qui baptizarent et exhortarent populum indigentem et desiderantem, sicut Dominus inquit in euangelio, admonet et docet dicens: 'Euntes ergo nunc docete omnes gentes baptizantes eas in nomine Patris et Filii et Spiritus Sancti docentes eos obseruare omnia quaecumque mandaui uobis: et ecce ego uobiscum sum omnibus diebus usque ad consummationem saeculi', et iterum dicit 'Euntes ergo in mundum uniuersum praedicate euangelium omni creaturae; qui crediderit et baptizatus fuerit saluus erit; qui uero non crediderit condempnabitur' et iterum 'Praedicabitur hoc euangelium regni in uniuerso mundo in testimonium omnibus gentibus et tunc ueniet finis' et item Dominus per prophetam praenuntiat, inquit 'Et erit in nouissimis diebus, dicit Dominus, effundam de Spiritu meo super omnem carnem et prophetabunt filii uestri et filiae uestrae et iuuenes uestri uisiones uidebunt et seniores uestri somnia somniabunt et quidem super seruos meos et super ancillas meas in diebus illis effundam de Spiritu meo et prophetabunt', et 'in Osee dicit, Uocabo non plebem meam plebem meam et non misericordiam consecutam misericordiam consecutam et erit in loco ubi dictum est, Non plebs mea uos, ibi uocabuntur filii Dei uiui.'

Unde autem Hiberione qui numquam notitiam Dei habuerunt nisi idola et inmunda usque nunc semper coluerunt quomodo 'nuper facta est plebs Domini' et filii Dei nuncupantur, filii Scottorum et filiae regulorum monachi et uirgines Xpisti esse uidentur? Et etiam una benedicta Scotta genetiua nobilis pulcherrima adulta erat, quam ego baptizaui, et post paucos dies una causa uenit ad nos, insinuauit nobis responsum accepisse a nuntio Dei et monuit eam ut esset uirgo Xpisti et ipsa Deo proximaret: Deo gratias, sexta ab hac die optime et auidissime arripuit illud quod etiam omnes uirgines Dei ita hoc faciunt, non sponte patrum earum, sed et persecutiones patiuntur et improperia falsa a parentibus suis et nihilominus plus augetur numerus, et de genere nostro qui ibi nati sunt, nescimus numerum eorum, praeter uiduas et continentes. Sed et illae maxime laborant quae seruitio detinentur, usque ad terrores et minas assidue perferunt; sed Dominus gratiam dedit multis ex ancillis suis, nam etsi uetantur tamen fortiter imitantur.

Unde autem etsi uoluero amittere illas et ut pergens in Brittanniis, et libentissime 'paratus eram' quasi ad patriam et parentes; non id solum sed etiam usque ad Gallias uisitare fratres et ut uiderem faciem sanctorum Domini mei; scit Deus quod ego ualde optabam, sed 'alligatus Spiritu', qui mihi 'protestatur' si hoc fecero, ut futurum reum me esse designat et timeo perdere laborem quem inchoaui, et non ego sed Xpistus Dominus, qui me imperauit ut uenirem esse cum illis residuum aetatis meae, 'si Dominus uoluerit' et custodierit me ab omni uia mala, ut non 'peccem coram illo'.

Spero autem hoc debueram, sed memet ipsum non credo 'quamdiu fuero in hoc corpore mortis', quia fortis est qui cotidie nititur subuertere me a fide et praeposita castitate religionis non fictae usque in finem uitae meae Xpisto Domino meo, sed 'caro inimica' semper trahit ad mortem, id est ad inlecebras inlicitate perficiendas; et 'scio ex parte' quare uitam perfectam ego non egi 'sicut' et 'ceteri' credentes, sed confiteor Domino meo, et non erubesco in conspectu ipsius 'quia non mentior' ex quo cognoui eum 'a iuuentute mea' creuit in me amor Dei et timor ipsius 'et usque nunc' fauente Domino 'fidem seruaui'. Rideat autem et insultet qui uoluerit, ego non silebo neque abscondo signa et mirabilia quae mihi a Domino monstrata sunt ante multos annos quam fierent, quasi qui nouit omnia etiam 'ante tempora saecularia'.

Unde autem debueram sine cessatione Deo gratias agere, qui saepe indulsit insipientiae meae neglegentiae meae et de loco non in uno quoque ut non mihi uehementer irasceretur, qui adiutor datus sum et non cito adquieui secundum quod mihi ostensum fuerat et sicut 'Spiritus suggerebat' et 'misertus est' mihi Dominus 'in milia milium', quia uidit in me quod 'paratus eram', sed quod mihi pro his nesciebam de statu meo quid facerem, quia multi hanc legationem prohibebant, etiam inter se ipsos post tergum meum narrabant et dicebant "Iste quare se mittit in periculo inter hostes qui Deum non nouerunt?" non ut causa malitiae, sed non sapiebat illis, sicut et ego ipse testor, intellegi propter rusticitatem meam, et non cito agnoui gratiam quae tunc erat in me; nunc mihi sapit quod ante debueram.

Nunc ergo simpliciter insinuaui fratribus et conseruis meis qui mihi crediderunt propter quod 'praedixi et praedico' ad roborandum et confirmandam fidem uestram. Utinam ut et uos imitemini maiora et potiora faciatis. Hoc erit gloria mea, quia 'filius sapiens gloria patris est'. Uos scitis et Deus qualiter inter uos conuersatus sum 'a iuuentute mea' in fide ueritatis 'et in sinceritate cordis'. Etiam ad gentes illas inter quas habito, ego fidem illis praestaui et praestabo. Deus scit 'neminem' illorum 'circumueni', nec cogito, propter Deum et ecclesiam ipsius, ne 'excitem' illis et nobis omnibus 'persecutionem' et ne per me blasphemaretur nomen Domini, quia scriptum est 'Uae homini per quem nomen Domini blasphematur'. Nam 'etsi imperitus sum in omnibus' tamen conatus sum quippiam seruare me etiam et fratribus Xpistianis et uirginibus Xpisti et mulieribus religiosis, quae mihi ultronea munuscula donabant et super altare iactabant ex ornamentis suis et iterum reddebam illis et aduersus me scandalizabantur cur hoc faciebam.

Sed ego propter spem perennitatis, ut me in omnibus caute propterea conseruarem, ita ut non me in aliquo titulo infideli caperent uel ministerium seruitutis meae nec etiam in minimo incredulis locum darem infamare siue detractare. Forte autem quando baptizaui tot milia hominum sperauerim ab aliquo illorum uel dimidio scriptulae? 'Dicite mihi et reddam uobis.' Aut quando ordinauit ubique Dominus clericos per modicitatem meam et ministerium gratis distribui illis si poposci ab aliquo illorum uel pretium uel 'calciamenti' mei, 'dicite aduersus me et reddam uobis' magis. Ego 'impendi pro' uobis ut me 'caperent', et inter uos et ubique pergebam causa uestra in multis periculis etiam usque ad exteras partes, ubi nemo ultra erat et ubi numquam aliquis peruenerat qui baptizaret aut clericos ordinaret aut populum consummaret, donante Domino diligenter et libentissime pro salute uestra omnia generaui. Interim praemia dabam regibus praeter quod dabam mercedem filiis ipsorum qui mecum ambulant, et nihilominus comprehenderunt me cum comitibus meis et illa die auidissime cupiebant interficere me, sed tempus nondum uenerat et omnia quaecumque nobiscum inuenerunt rapuerunt illud et me ipsum ferro uinxerunt et quartodecimo die absoluit me Dominus de potestate eorum et quicquid nostrum fuit redditum est nobis propter Deum et 'necessarios amicos' quos ante praeuidimus. Uos autem experti estis quantum ego erogaui illis qui iudicabant 'per omnes regiones' quos ego frequentius uisitabam. Censeo enim non minimum quam pretium quindecim hominum distribui illis, ita ut me 'fruamini' et ego 'uobis' semper 'fruar' in Deum. Non me paenitet nec satis est mihi: adhuc 'impendo et superimpendam'; potens est Dominus ut det mihi postmodum ut meipsum 'impendar pro animabus uestris'.

Ecce 'testem Deum inuoco in animam meam quia non mentior': neque ut sit 'occasio adulationis' uel 'auaritiae' scripserim uobis neque ut honorem spero ab aliquo uestro; sufficit enim honor qui nondum uidetur sed corde creditur; 'fidelis' autem 'qui promisit: numquam mentitur'.

Sed uideo iam 'in praesenti saeculo' me supra modum exaltatum a Domino, et non eram dignus neque talis ut hoc mihi praestaret, dum scio certissime quod mihi melius conuenit paupertas et calamitas quam diuitiae et diliciae, sed et Xpistus Dominus pauper' fuit 'pro nobis', ego uero miser et infelix etsi opes uoluero iam non habeo, 'neque me ipsum iudico', quia cotidie spero aut internicionem aut circumueniri aut redigi in seruitutem siue occasio cuiuslibet, 'sed nihil horum uereor' propter promissa caelorum, quia iactaui meipsum in manus Dei omnipotentis, qui ubique dominatur.

Sicut propheta dicit 'Iacta cogitatum tuum in Deum et ipse te enutriet'. Ecce nunc 'commendo animam meam fidelissimo Deo' meo, 'pro quo legationem fungor' in ignobilitate mea, sed quia 'personam non accipit' et elegit me ad hoc officium ut 'unus' essem 'de suis minimis' minister.

Unde autem 'retribuam illi pro omnibus quae retribuit mihi'. Sed quid dicam uel quid promittam Domino meo, quia nihil ualeo nisi ipse mihi dederit? Sed 'scrutatur corda et renes' quia satis et nimis cupio et 'paratus eram' ut donaret mihi 'bibere calicem' eius, sicut indulsit et ceteris amantibus se. Quapropter non contingat mihi a Deo meo ut numquam amittam 'plebem' suam 'quam adquisiuit' in ultimis terrae. Oro Deum ut det mihi perseuerantiam et dignetur ut reddam illi testem fidelem usque ad transitum meum propter Deum meum, et si aliquid boni umquam imitatus sum propter Deum meum, quem diligo, peto illi det mihi ut cum illis proselitis et captiuis pro nomine suo effundam sanguinem meum, etsi ipsam etiam caream sepulturam aut miserissime cadauer per singula membra diuidatur canibus aut bestiis asperis aut 'uolucres caeli comederent illud'. Certissime reor, si mihi hoc incurrisset, lucratus sum animam cum corpore meo, quia 'sine ulla dubitatione' in die illa 'resurgemus' in claritate solis, hoc est 'in gloria' Xpisti Iesu redemptoris nostri, quasi 'filii Dei' uiui et 'coheredes Xpisti' et 'conformes futuri imaginis ipsius'; quoniam 'ex ipso et per ipsum et in ipso' regnaturi sumus. Nam sol iste quem uidemus ipso iubente propter nos cotidie oritur, sed numquam regnabit neque permanebit splendor eius, sed et omnes qui adorant eum in poenam miseri male deuenient; nos autem qui credimus et adoramus solem uerum Xpistum, qui numquam interibit neque 'qui fecerit uoluntatem' ipsius, sed 'manebit in aeternum quomodo et Xpistus manet in aeternum', qui regnat cum Deo Patre Omnipotente et cum Spiritu Sancto ante saecula et nunc et per omnia saecula saeculorum. Amen.

Ecce iterum iterumque breuiter exponam uerba Confessionis meae. 'Testificor' in ueritate et in 'exultatione cordis coram Deo et sanctis angelis eius' quia numquam habui aliquam occasionem praeter euangelium et promissa illius ut umquam redirem ad gentem illam unde prius uix euaseram.

Sed precor credentibus et timentibus Deum, quicumque dignatus fuerit inspicere uel recipere hanc scripturam quam Patricius peccator indoctus scilicet Hiberione conscripsit, ut nemo umquam dicat quod mea ignorantia, si aliquid pusillum egi uel demonstrauerim secundum Dei placitum, sed arbitramini et uerissime credatur quod 'donum Dei' fuisset. Et haec est Confessio mea antequam moriar.